William Shakespeare

MACBETH

Edited with a Commentary by George Hunter
Introduced by Carol Chillington Rutter

PENGUIN BOOKS

PENGUIN BOOKS

Published by the Penguin Group
Penguin Books Ltd, 80 Strand, London WC2R ORL, England
Penguin Group (USA) Inc., 375 Hudson Street, New York, New York 10014, USA
Penguin Group (Canada), 10 Alcorn Avenue, Toronto, Ontario, Canada M4V 3B2
(a division of Pearson Penguin Canada Inc.)
Penguin Ireland, 25 St Stephen's Green, Dublin 2, Ireland (a division of Penguin Books Ltd)
Penguin Group (Australia), 250 Camberwell Road, Camberwell, Victoria 3124, Australia
(a division of Pearson Australia Group Pty Ltd)
Penguin Books India Pvt Ltd, 11 Community Centre, Panchsheel Park, New Delhi – 110 017, India
Penguin Group (NZ), cnr Airborne and Rosedale Roads, Albany, Auckland 1310, New Zealand
(a division of Pearson New Zealand Ltd)
Penguin Books (South Africa) (Pty) Ltd, 24 Sturdee Avenue, Rosebank 2196, South Africa

Penguin Books Ltd, Registered Offices: 80 Strand, London WC2R ORL, England

www.penguin.com

This edition first published in Penguin Books 1967
Reissued in the Penguin Shakespeare series 2005

6

Account of the Text and Commentary copyright © George Hunter, 1967, 1995
General Introduction and Chronology copyright © Stanley Wells, 2005
Introduction and The Play in Performance copyright © Carol Chillington Rutter, 2005
Further Reading copyright © George Hunter, 1995; updated by Carol Chillington Rutter, 2005

Set in 11.5/12.5 PostScript Monotype Fournier
Typeset by Palimpsest Book Production Limited, Polmont, Stirlingshire
Printed in England by Clays Ltd, St Ives plc

ISBN-13: 978-0-141-01369-5

www.greenpenguin.co.uk

Penguin Books is committed to a sustainable future
for our business, our readers and our planet.
The book in your hands is made from paper
certified by the Forest Stewardship Council.

Contents

General Introduction

Every play by Shakespeare is unique. This is part of his greatness. A restless and indefatigable experimenter, he moved with a rare amalgamation of artistic integrity and dedicated professionalism from one kind of drama to another. Never shackled by convention, he offered his actors the alternation between serious and comic modes from play to play, and often also within the plays themselves, that the repertory system within which he worked demanded, and which provided an invaluable stimulus to his imagination. Introductions to individual works in this series attempt to define their individuality. But there are common factors that underpin Shakespeare's career.

Nothing in his heredity offers clues to the origins of his genius. His upbringing in Stratford-upon-Avon, where he was born in 1564, was unexceptional. His mother, born Mary Arden, came from a prosperous farming family. Her father chose her as his executor over her eight sisters and his four stepchildren when she was only in her late teens, which suggests that she was of more than average practical ability. Her husband John, a glover, apparently unable to write, was nevertheless a capable businessman and loyal townsfellow, who seems to have fallen on relatively hard times in later life. He would have been brought up as a Catholic, and may have retained

Catholic sympathies, but his son subscribed publicly to Anglicanism throughout his life.

The most important formative influence on Shakespeare was his school. As the son of an alderman who became bailiff (or mayor) in 1568, he had the right to attend the town's grammar school. Here he would have received an education grounded in classical rhetoric and oratory, studying authors such as Ovid, Cicero and Quintilian, and would have been required to read, speak, write and even think in Latin from his early years. This classical education permeates Shakespeare's work from the beginning to the end of his career. It is apparent in the self-conscious classicism of plays of the early 1590s such as the tragedy of *Titus Andronicus*, *The Comedy of Errors*, and the narrative poems *Venus and Adonis* (1592–3) and *The Rape of Lucrece* (1593–4), and is still evident in his latest plays, informing the dream visions of *Pericles* and *Cymbeline* and the masque in *The Tempest*, written between 1607 and 1611. It inflects his literary style throughout his career. In his earliest writings the verse, based on the ten-syllabled, five-beat iambic pentameter, is highly patterned. Rhetorical devices deriving from classical literature, such as alliteration and antithesis, extended similes and elaborate wordplay, abound. Often, as in *Love's Labour's Lost* and *A Midsummer Night's Dream*, he uses rhyming patterns associated with lyric poetry, each line self-contained in sense, the prose as well as the verse employing elaborate figures of speech. Writing at a time of linguistic ferment, Shakespeare frequently imports Latinisms into English, coining words such as abstemious, addiction, incarnadine and adjunct. He was also heavily influenced by the eloquent translations of the Bible in both the Bishops' and the Geneva versions. As his experience grows, his verse and prose become more supple, the patterning less apparent, more ready to accommodate the rhythms of ordinary speech, more colloquial in diction, as in the speeches of the Nurse in *Romeo and Juliet*, the characterful prose of Falstaff and Hamlet's soliloquies. The effect is of increasing psychological realism, reaching its greatest heights in *Hamlet*, *Othello*, *King Lear*, *Macbeth* and *Antony and Cleopatra*. Gradually he discovered ways of adapting the regular beat of the pentameter to make it an infinitely flexible instrument for matching thought with feeling. Towards the end of his career, in plays such as *The Winter's Tale*, *Cymbeline* and *The Tempest*, he adopts a more highly mannered style, in keeping with the more overtly symbolical and emblematical mode in which he is writing.

So far as we know, Shakespeare lived in Stratford till after his marriage to Anne Hathaway, eight years his senior, in 1582. They had three children: a daughter, Susanna, born in 1583 within six months of their marriage, and twins, Hamnet and Judith, born in 1585. The next seven years of Shakespeare's life are virtually a blank. Theories that he may have been, for instance, a schoolmaster, or a lawyer, or a soldier, or a sailor, lack evidence to support them. The first reference to him in print, in Robert Greene's pamphlet *Greene's Groatsworth of Wit* of 1592, parodies a line from *Henry VI, Part III*, implying that Shakespeare was already an established playwright. It seems likely that at some unknown point after the birth of his twins he joined a theatre company and gained experience as both actor and writer in the provinces and London. The London theatres closed because of plague in 1593 and 1594; and during these years, perhaps recognizing the need for an alternative career, he wrote and published the narrative poems *Venus and Adonis* and *The Rape of Lucrece*. These are the only works we can be certain that Shakespeare himself was responsible for putting into print. Each bears the author's dedication to Henry Wriothesley, Earl of Southampton (1573–1624), the second in warmer terms than the first. Southampton, younger than Shakespeare by ten years, is the only person to whom he personally dedicated works. The Earl may have been a close friend, perhaps even the beautiful and adored young man whom Shakespeare celebrates in his *Sonnets*.

The resumption of playing after the plague years saw the founding of the Lord Chamberlain's Men, a company to which Shakespeare was to belong for the rest of his career, as actor, shareholder and playwright. No other dramatist of the period had so stable a relationship with a single company. Shakespeare knew the actors for whom he was writing and the conditions in which they performed. The permanent company was made up of around twelve to fourteen players, but one actor often played more than one role in a play and additional actors were hired as needed. Led by the tragedian Richard Burbage (1568–1619) and, initially, the comic actor Will Kemp (d. 1603), they rapidly achieved a high reputation, and when King James I succeeded Queen Elizabeth I in 1603 they were renamed as the King's Men. All the women's parts were played by boys; there is no evidence that any female role was ever played by a male actor over the age of about eighteen. Shakespeare had enough confidence in his boys to write for them long and demanding roles such as Rosalind (who, like other heroines of the romantic comedies, is disguised as a boy for much of the action) in *As You Like It*, Lady Macbeth and Cleopatra. But there are far more fathers than mothers, sons than daughters, in his plays, few if any of which require more than the company's normal complement of three or four boys.

The company played primarily in London's public playhouses – there were almost none that we know of in the rest of the country – initially in the Theatre, built in Shoreditch in 1576, and from 1599 in the Globe, on Bankside. These were wooden, more or less circular structures, open to the air, with a thrust stage surmounted by a canopy and jutting into the area where spectators who paid one penny stood, and surrounded by galleries where it was possible to be seated on payment of an additional penny. Though properties such as cauldrons, stocks, artificial trees or beds could indicate locality, there was no representational scenery. Sound effects such as flourishes of trumpets, music both martial and amorous, and accompaniments to songs were provided by the company's musicians. Actors entered through doors in the back wall of the stage. Above it was a balconied area that could represent the walls of a town (as in *King John*), or a castle (as in *Richard II*), and indeed a balcony (as in *Romeo and Juliet*). In 1609 the company also acquired the use of the Blackfriars, a smaller, indoor theatre to which admission was more expensive, and which permitted the use of more spectacular stage effects such as the descent of Jupiter on an eagle in *Cymbeline* and of goddesses in *The Tempest*. And they would frequently perform before the court in royal residences and, on their regular tours into the provinces, in non-theatrical spaces such as inns, guild-halls and the great halls of country houses.

Early in his career Shakespeare may have worked in collaboration, perhaps with Thomas Nashe (1567–*c*. 1601) in *Henry VI, Part I* and with George Peele (1556–96) in *Titus Andronicus*. And towards the end he collaborated with George Wilkins (*fl*. 1604–8) in *Pericles*, and with his younger colleagues Thomas Middleton (1580–1627), in *Timon of Athens*, and John Fletcher (1579–1625), in *Henry*

VIII, *The Two Noble Kinsmen* and the lost play *Cardenio*.
Shakespeare's output dwindled in his last years, and he
died in 1616 in Stratford, where he owned a fine house,
New Place, and much land. His only son had died at the
age of eleven, in 1596, and his last descendant died in
1670. New Place was destroyed in the eighteenth century
but the other Stratford houses associated with his life are
maintained and displayed to the public by the Shakespeare
Birthplace Trust.

One of the most remarkable features of Shakespeare's
plays is their intellectual and emotional scope. They span
a great range from the lightest of comedies, such as *The
Two Gentlemen of Verona* and *The Comedy of Errors*, to
the profoundest of tragedies, such as *King Lear* and
Macbeth. He maintained an output of around two plays
a year, ringing the changes between comic and serious.
All his comedies have serious elements: Shylock, in *The
Merchant of Venice*, almost reaches tragic dimensions, and
Measure for Measure is profoundly serious in its examin-
ation of moral problems. Equally, none of his tragedies
is without humour: Hamlet is as witty as any of his comic
heroes, *Macbeth* has its Porter, and *King Lear* its Fool.
His greatest comic character, Falstaff, inhabits the history
plays and *Henry V* ends with a marriage, while *Henry
VI, Part III*, *Richard II* and *Richard III* culminate in the
tragic deaths of their protagonists.

Although in performance Shakespeare's characters can
give the impression of a superabundant reality, he is not
a naturalistic dramatist. None of his plays is explicitly
set in his own time. The action of few of them (except
for the English histories) is set even partly in England
(exceptions are *The Merry Wives of Windsor* and the
Induction to *The Taming of the Shrew*). Italy is his
favoured location. Most of his principal story-lines derive

from printed writings; but the structuring and translation of these narratives into dramatic terms is Shakespeare's own, and he invents much additional material. Most of the plays contain elements of myth and legend, and many derive from ancient or more recent history or from romantic tales of ancient times and faraway places. All reflect his reading, often in close detail. Holinshed's *Chronicles* (1577, revised 1587), a great compendium of English, Scottish and Irish history, provided material for his English history plays. The *Lives of the Noble Grecians and Romans* by the Greek writer Plutarch, finely translated into English from the French by Sir Thomas North in 1579, provided much of the narrative material, and also a mass of verbal detail, for his plays about Roman history. Some plays are closely based on shorter individual works: *As You Like It*, for instance, on the novel *Rosalynde* (1590) by his near-contemporary Thomas Lodge (1558–1625), *The Winter's Tale* on *Pandosto* (1588) by his old rival Robert Greene (1558–92) and *Othello* on a story by the Italian Giraldi Cinthio (1504–73). And the language of his plays is permeated by the Bible, the Book of Common Prayer and the proverbial sayings of his day.

Shakespeare was popular with his contemporaries, but his commitment to the theatre and to the plays in performance is demonstrated by the fact that only about half of his plays appeared in print in his lifetime, in slim paperback volumes known as quartos, so called because they were made from printers' sheets folded twice to form four leaves (eight pages). None of them shows any sign that he was involved in their publication. For him, performance was the primary means of publication. The most frequently reprinted of his works were the nondramatic poems – the erotic *Venus and Adonis* and the more moralistic *The Rape of Lucrece*. The *Sonnets*, which appeared in 1609, under his name but possibly without his consent, were less successful, perhaps because the vogue for sonnet sequences, which peaked in the 1590s, had passed by then. They were not reprinted until 1640, and then only in garbled form along with poems by other writers. Happily, in 1623, seven years after he died, his colleagues John Heminges (1556–1630) and Henry Condell (d. 1627) published his collected plays, including eighteen that had not previously appeared in print, in the first Folio, whose name derives from the fact that the printers' sheets were folded only once to produce two leaves (four pages). Some of the quarto editions are badly printed, and the fact that some plays exist in two, or even three, early versions creates problems for editors. These are discussed in the Account of the Text in each volume of this series.

Shakespeare's plays continued in the repertoire until the Puritans closed the theatres in 1642. When performances resumed after the Restoration of the monarchy in 1660 many of the plays were not to the taste of the times, especially because their mingling of genres and failure to meet the requirements of poetic justice offended against the dictates of neoclassicism. Some, such as *The Tempest* (changed by John Dryden and William Davenant in 1667 to suit contemporary taste), *King Lear* (to which Nahum Tate gave a happy ending in 1681) and *Richard III* (heavily adapted by Colley Cibber in 1700 as a vehicle for his own talents), were extensively rewritten; others fell into neglect. Slowly they regained their place in the repertoire, and they continued to be reprinted, but it was not until the great actor David Garrick (1717–79) organized a spectacular jubilee in Stratford in 1769 that Shakespeare began to be regarded as a transcendental genius. Garrick's idolatry prefigured the enthusiasm of critics such as Samuel Taylor Coleridge (1772–1834) and William Hazlitt (1778–1830). Gradually Shakespeare's reputation spread abroad, to Germany, America, France and to other European countries.

During the nineteenth century, though the plays were generally still performed in heavily adapted or abbreviated versions, a large body of scholarship and criticism began to amass. Partly as a result of a general swing in education away from the teaching of Greek and Roman texts and towards literature written in English, Shakespeare became the object of intensive study in schools and universities. In the theatre, important turning points were the work in England of two theatre directors, William Poel (1852–1934) and his disciple Harley Granville-Barker (1877–1946), who showed that the application of knowledge, some of it newly acquired, of early staging conditions to performance of the plays could render the original texts viable in terms of the modern theatre. During the twentieth century appreciation of Shakespeare's work, encouraged by the availability of audio, film and video versions of the plays, spread around the world to such an extent that he can now be claimed as a global author.

The influence of Shakespeare's works permeates the English language. Phrases from his plays and poems – 'a tower of strength', 'green-eyed jealousy', 'a foregone conclusion' – are on the lips of people who may never have read him. They have inspired composers of songs, orchestral music and operas; painters and sculptors; poets, novelists and film-makers. Allusions to him appear in pop songs, in advertisements and in television shows. Some of his characters – Romeo and Juliet, Falstaff, Shylock and Hamlet – have acquired mythic status. He is valued for his humanity, his psychological insight, his wit and humour, his lyricism, his mastery of language, his ability to excite, surprise, move and, in the widest sense of the word, entertain audiences. He is the greatest of poets, but he is essentially a dramatic poet. Though his plays have much to offer to readers, they exist fully only in performance. In these volumes we offer individual introductions, notes on language and on specific points of the text, suggestions for further reading and information about how each work has been edited. In addition we include accounts of the ways in which successive generations of interpreters and audiences have responded to challenges and rewards offered by the plays. The Penguin Shakespeare series aspires to remove obstacles to understanding and to make pleasurable the reading of the work of the man who has done more than most to make us understand what it is to be human.

Stanley Wells

The Chronology of Shakespeare's Works

A few of Shakespeare's writings can be fairly precisely dated. An allusion to the Earl of Essex in the chorus to Act V of *Henry V*, for instance, could only have been written in 1599. But for many of the plays we have only vague information, such as the date of publication, which may have occurred long after composition, the date of a performance, which may not have been the first, or a list in Francis Meres's book *Palladis Tamia*, published in 1598, which tells us only that the plays listed there must have been written by that year. The chronology of the early plays is particularly difficult to establish. Not everyone would agree that the first part of *Henry VI* was written after the third, for instance, or *Romeo and Juliet* before *A Midsummer Night's Dream*. The following table is based on the 'Canon and Chronology' section in *William Shakespeare: A Textual Companion*, by Stanley Wells and Gary Taylor, with John Jowett and William Montgomery (1987), where more detailed information and discussion may be found.

The Two Gentlemen of Verona	1590–91
The Taming of the Shrew	1590–91
Henry VI, Part II	1591
Henry VI, Part III	1591

Introduction

What kind of feeling is fear? A stimulant, like adrenalin, or a sedative, an anaesthetic that deadens our conscience? Does it save us from disaster or prompt us to folly – or does it just get in the way of our ambitions? Fear might be the red flag that tells us 'Proceed no further!', like Laertes warning his sister that Prince Hamlet's love is dangerous: 'Fear it, Ophelia, fear it' (I.3.33). Or it might be the white feather that tells us we are chicken, too scared to take the dare – any dare, like 'pigeon-livered' Hamlet ducking out of the instruction to 'Revenge!' (II.2.574). Absurdly, when we have nothing to fear, we humans *invent* fears. We make terrors of trifles and frighten ourselves to death with them – a syndrome Theseus in *A Midsummer Night's Dream* diagnoses (and mocks): 'in the night, imagining some fear, | How easy is a bush supposed a bear!' (V.1.21–2). Making bears of bushes in broad daylight, however, is probably an early symptom of paranoia.

These speculations are pertinent to *Macbeth*. In *Macbeth* we grow familiar with fear, learn to hear, taste, see, feel it on the backs of our necks, at the ends of our fingers and in the centres of our brains. For *Macbeth* is Shakespeare's most fear-full play, his anatomy of fear. The word appears here more often than anywhere else in his work, and along with it, its now-redundant seventeenth-century synonym 'doubt', which means not only 'to be uncertain', 'to hesitate to believe or trust' but also 'to dread, fear, be afraid of '. In *Macbeth* soldiers fear their closest comrades; subjects their king; wives their husbands, fearing their fear. Children fear toy monsters and painted devils; birds fear nets. Everyone fears rumour – and what they 'know not'. Nightwalkers fear noises: footsteps on stone, the owl's shriek, someone knocking at the gate. Eyes fear to look at what hands have done, and memory fears to remember what no known medicine can scour from hurt minds, from scorpion-infested brains. (Once initiated, however, hands grow hardened to fear, and tongues grow used to its rancid taste in the mouth.) Hosts fear guests who, invited, are not expected to turn up to the feast they nevertheless attend. Awake, men fear nightmare hallucinations; asleep, 'the affliction' of 'terrible dreams' that 'shake us nightly' (III.2.18–19). Servants doubt the approach of danger. Their masters doubt equivocation. All who depend on language learn to doubt its doubleness. Why does he 'start, and seem to fear | Things that do sound so fair?' asks Banquo when Macbeth recoils from the Weird Sisters' prophetic greetings at I.3.50–51. The rest of the play works to answer that question, an answer made all the trickier by the fact that 'fear' and 'fair', so distinct to our hearing as to be opposites, are, as George Hunter in his Commentary reminds us, acoustic twins to Jacobean ears. 'Fear' and 'fair' were 'pronounced alike in Shakespeare's day' (see note to I.3.50–51). And Macbeth himself is the original 'fair' whom the play learns to 'fear'.

In simplest terms *Macbeth* is the story of a man who releases fear into his world. He is a soldier, expert at battlefield killing, who commits murder, killing a sleeping man, killing him at home. And when the murder is done, he learns what doing it means by suffering its consequences.

Macbeth is not rash in killing. Indeed, he is the most brooding, the most premeditating of Shakespeare's tragic players. (It is worth remembering that Shakespeare's tragic protagonists – Hamlet, Lear, Othello, Titus, Brutus, Antony, Romeo, Coriolanus – are not men who have mighty flaws but men who make mighty mistakes.) Macbeth is not unwitting, rash, confused or clumsy. He cannot claim with King Lear, 'I am a man | More sinned against than sinning' (III.2.59–60). Or with Romeo, 'I thought all for the best' (III.1.104). He does not rationalize killing as something else, revenge, for instance, as Hamlet does, or piety, as Titus does. Nor for him is killing the execution of justice, a terrible but necessary sacrifice, like Othello, persuaded that Desdemona 'must die, else she'll betray more men' (V.2.6). Macbeth, by contrast, knows that what he is contemplating is murder, and knows the murder of Duncan is wrong. He calls it 'deep damnation', a 'horrid deed' (I.7.20, 24). He even knows the best reason not to kill. The murderer is a suicide. The murderer teaches 'Bloody instructions, which, being taught, return | To plague the inventor'; he 'Commends the ingredience' of the 'poisoned chalice' to his 'own lips' (9–12).

If he is the most thoughtful, he is also the most heinous of Shakespeare's 'mighty mistakers', the only one who, 'By the worst means' pursues 'the worst' (III.4.134). Macbeth is a regicide, a king-killer. Killing a king is a political crime, but it is also a crime against family, that is, a dynastic crime. And as *Macbeth* gives us terms to understand, it is a crime ultimately against the universe, its horror finding adequate expression only in universal, organic and religious imagery, for the King, alive, expresses the kingdom's *live*liness, its fertility, its growth and continuance. 'I have begun to plant thee,' Duncan tells Macbeth, embracing the hero-warrior who has saved his throne from overthrow by rebels, 'and will labour | To make thee full of growing' (I.4.29–30); 'our duties . . . to your throne and state,' Macbeth observes, are 'children and servants, | Which do but what they should by doing everything | Safe toward your love and honour' (25–8). To kill a king is to mock love, cancel duty's contract, to rend the bond of nature, to hack down the tree of life. Duncan, murdered, is 'The Lord's anointed temple' broken open and sacked; 'his gashed stabs' look 'like a breach in nature | For ruin's wasteful entrance' (II.3.65, 110–11). In *Macbeth* no concealment of this appalling double rupture – of the King's body natural and his symbolic body – is possible. The cosmos, in revulsion, will go to extravagant lengths to make the crime known. Strange alliances between things physical and psychical, natural and supernatural, will produce terrifying instruments of revelation: angels will trumpet the truth, posting around the globe on the blind horseback of uproar's storm, and 'Pity, like a naked new-born babe | Striding the blast' will 'blow the horrid deed in every eye, | That tears shall drown the wind' (I.7.21–5). Men will know how to read these cosmic signs when, right on their own doorsteps, they see nature turned upside down, when there is darkness on earth instead of daylight; when falcons are 'hawked at and killed' by 'mousing' owls; when Duncan's horses turn 'wild in nature', break their stalls – and eat each other (II.4.13, 16).

Worse even, though, than a killer of kings, Macbeth is a killer of children. In this play children's bodies, like the King's, play double. They perform both actual and

symbolic functions, which makes it doubly significant
that unlike Duncan, Banquo, Macduff and Seyward (all
the grown men of the play), Macbeth has no children.
Childless, his barrenness mocks his dynastic project,
emptying it of any future meaning beyond his own ambition to wear the crown. When he is brooding upon the
murder beforehand, Macbeth fixes upon his chances of
getting away with it, calculating whether 'the assassination' will 'trammel up the consequence' – a trammel being
a net – 'and catch | With his surcease success' (I.7.2–4).
Only later does he understand that he made the wrong
calculation, that it is not 'surcease' – making an end,
killing Duncan – that delivers 'success' but *'succession'*.
There can be no 'success' (that is, 'good outcome' but
also 'sequel') without 'succession' (an heir, issue, someone
to succeed him). To have no children means the death of
ambition: as children fail Macbeth, Macbeth's future fails.
And if that happens, Lady Macbeth is right: 'Naught's
had, all's spent' (III.2.4). Macbeth wears a 'fruitless
crown' and grips a 'barren sceptre' (III.1.60–61). He has
'Put rancours in the vessel of [his] peace' and given his
'eternal jewel' to 'the common enemy of man', his soul
to Satan, to make *'them* kings', the sons 'of Banquo kings'
(66–9). To stop the future, Macbeth must stop the children – by slaughtering them. But childlessness, even if
it is traumatically frustrating to Macbeth, is something
he sees only in dynastic terms. It means much, much
more to Macduff. It is the only explanation Macduff can
give for Macbeth's crime when he learns that the 'hell-
kite' (IV.3.217) has surprised his castle and wasted his
entire family – 'Wife, children, servants, all | That could
be found': 'He has no children', says Macduff, numbly,
dumbly in response (211–12, 215). It seems so little to say,
in the event. Almost nothing. But that in itself registers

Macduff's attempt to express what for him is inexpressible: how can a man who has no children understand what it means to kill a child? A child-killer is not just hacking at the tree of life. He is spilling 'nature's germens', tumbling the seeds of life into ruined wastefulness, making 'destruction sicken' (IV.1.58–9).

So given this appalling history, how is it that, by the end of the play, we see the roles of butcher and butchered reversed – and Macbeth the *victim* of the tragedy? How is it that he is no longer a ranging wolf or a swooping hell-kite but a bear tied to a stake, savaged by hounds; no longer the slaughterman of all the children but a grieving husband bereft of 'that which should accompany old age', 'honour, love, obedience, troops of friends' (V.3.24–5); no longer the 'peerless kinsman' but a 'poor player' whose life is 'a tale | Told by an idiot', 'Signifying nothing' (I.4.59; V.5.24, 26–8)? How is it that we feel not satisfaction at the end but sorrow? Or to put the question differently, how does *Macbeth* end as tragedy, not melodrama? And are all these questions somehow attached to the ones Macbeth puts in his opening scene to those 'imperfect speakers' (I.3.69), the Weird Sisters, who tell him the future but do not stay to answer his interrogations? 'What are you?' he demands of the 'withered' 'wild' things who interrupt his first entrance, blocking his path by suddenly materializing out of the storm on the battle-churned heath, who 'look not like the inhabitants o'the earth, | And yet are on't' (38–46):

>   Say from whence
> You owe this strange intelligence; or why
> Upon this blasted heath you stop our way
> With such prophetic greeting? (74–7)

What? Whence? *Why?* (Why? is the question tragedy never answers; indeed, it is the unanswered question that lets us know we are *in* tragedy.) In the theatre, and in the text, we know more than Macbeth does at this moment. We know that he is keeping an appointment on the heath that he did not know he had arranged. We know that, out of battle's danger zone, headed for the safety of home, the warrior who has been stopped in his tracks by a chance encounter with strangers is being offered a 'suggestion' (133) that will change his life. For we know Macbeth is conversing with witches – and it is the material fact of those witches, those 'imperfect speakers', as the original happening in Macbeth's play that makes all the difference to the future they foretell.

HISTORY TEXTS / THEATRE TEXTS

Shakespeare found Macbeth, Duncan and the Weird Sisters in the second volume of Raphael Holinshed's *Chronicles* (1587). In fact 'Vol. II' gave him *two* records from Scotland's ancient past – legend or history? – to raid for material. In the earlier story Donwald, King Duff's 'captain of the castle', begs the lives of certain kinsmen who have been sentenced as traitors. Their crime was capital, but they were dupes, 'persuaded' through 'fraudulent counsel of diverse wicked persons': they were witches' stooges. So when Duff denies pardon, Donwald is outraged. Malice 'boiling in his stomach', he yields to his wife's persuasions when she shows how they might 'secretly cut' Duff's 'throat as he lay sleeping, without any buskling at all'.

The later, fuller story is set in the reign of King Duncan, a man 'so soft and gentle of nature', so 'negligent' in 'punishing offenders' that 'many misruled persons' take 'occasion thereof to trouble the peace and quiet state of the commonwealth' with 'seditious commotion'. First Macdowald rebels against the 'milksop', recruiting from Ireland 'no small number of Kernes and Galloglasses' who fight 'in hope of the spoil'. Next, Sueno of Norway invades. After him a Danish fleet attacks. In all these broils nothing daunts 'valiant Macbeth': he is as tough as his cousin-king (to whom he is next-in-blood) is tender. He sends Macdowald's head home to Duncan on a pole; surprises and slaughters Sueno's sleeping army; beats the Danes to the coast; then, with Banquo, heads towards Forres. But 'a strange and uncouth wonder' stops them: 'three women in strange and wild apparel, resembling creatures of the elder world' 'All hail' Macbeth 'thane of Glamis', 'thane of Cawdor', 'hereafter . . . king of Scotland'. Challenged by Banquo, they 'promise greater benefits' to him: not 'in deed' to reign but instead to father those who will. Then they vanish. Macbeth and Banquo laugh off the 'fantastical illusion' as 'jest'. But 'afterwards the common opinion was, that these women were either the weird sisters, that is (as you would say) the goddesses of destiny, or else some nymphs or fairies endued with knowledge of prophecy by their necromantical science, because every thing came to pass as they had spoken.'

It is not until some time later, however, that Macbeth makes his move to 'usurp the kingdom by force'. He remembers the 'words of the three sisters', but, even more crucially, listens to his wife. She 'lay sore upon him to attempt the thing' because she burned with an 'unquench-able desire to bear the name of a queen'. In Holinshed, Macbeth has 'just quarrel' against Duncan, and the killing is not the secret murder of a sleeping king. He enlists the aid of 'trusty friends' – chief among them, Banquo

– and kills Duncan in battle, afterwards reigning as a model ruler for a decade.

But this exemplary king is actually 'a counterfeit', living in constant 'fear', rankled by the witches' predictions. The 'prick of conscience' finally brings the real Macbeth into the open. Banquo is ambushed; Fleance flees; random assassinations follow; all Scotland suspects, fears, while Macbeth grows reckless in atrocities, assured that he is invulnerable until Birnam Wood climbs the hill to Dunsinane – or he meets a man not 'born of any woman'. Macduff rides to England to raise the resistance. Macbeth sends soldiers to Fife to wipe out his family. But Malcolm's army is mobilized. Macbeth retreats. Birnam Wood walks. The tyrant faces his last foe, mocks him with the witches' indemnity – and hears Macduff reply, 'I am even he', not 'born of my mother, but ripped out of her womb'. The rest of Macbeth's history is told in just five sentences. His head is set on a pole, like Macdowald's years before. And the *Chronicle* ends laconically: Macbeth 'accomplished many worthy acts' but, 'by illusion of the devil' – the first we have heard of *him* anywhere in this history – he 'defamed' his reign 'with most terrible cruelty'. He 'was slain in the year of the incarnation, 1057, and in the 16th year of King Edward's reign over the Englishmen'.

Reading Holinshed you can almost observe Shakespeare's mind passing over the *Chronicle* like a magnet picking up iron filings – images, exchanges, chance remarks that snag the memory. As he works upon this 'history text', the playwright telescopes time and condenses story, and, finding fear aplenty in Holinshed, lays out a moral universe where the line between 'the Good' and 'the Bad' seems to be firmly drawn. All the big ideas are there. What constitutes the 'good' ruler?

What are the 'king-becoming graces' (IV.3.91)? (The
material Shakespeare scripts in Act IV, scene 3, the
England scene, he lifts straight from Holinshed.) How
far is the man betrayed responsible for constructing the
traitor? What are the uses – and limits – of violence in
a culture where 'humane statute' has not yet 'purged the
gentle weal' (III.4.75)? What power do the 'instruments
of darkness' (I.3.123) wield in human life? Should men
listen to their wives – or to witches? How is Scotland –
with its renegade Irish, its blood-reeking warriors, its
feuding tribes, its 'weird sisters', its blasted, desolate landscape – how is Scotland a way of thinking about *England*?

We have no secure date either for the original writing
or first performance of *Macbeth*, but there were very
good reasons why Shakespeare may have wanted to
produce a 'Scottish play' in 1605 or 1606. James Stuart,
a Scot, the sixth of that house to reign in Scotland in a
dynasty that traced itself back to Banquo, inherited the
English throne when the last Tudor, Elizabeth, died in
1603. One of James's first moves was to take Shakespeare's playing company under his personal patronage,
rebranding the Chamberlain's Men 'the King's Men'.
Macbeth may have been Shakespeare's response to the
new arrangements; the play certainly picked up on topics
the King found absorbing.

James was interested in theories of government. In
1598, during an illness he feared he would not survive,
he wrote his political testament, a how-to manual for
monarchy, *Basilicon Doron* (the Kingly Gift), addressing
it to his four-year-old son, Henry. Divided into three
chapters, the book laid out the King's duty to God, his
office and himself, and offered instruction on everything
from administering justice, selecting counsellors and
choosing good books to managing churchmen, the

economy, marriage, his hair and his table manners. *Basilicon Doron* circulated widely in England after 1603, Englishmen scanning it as a kind of cipher decoding the unknown (and foreign) quantity that was their new King. Shakespeare may have read James on the difference between the good king and the tyrant: 'the one acknowledges himself ordained for his people, having received from God a burden of government whereof he must be accountable: the other thinks his people ordained for him, a prey to his appetites.' He may have paused over his remarks on diseased conscience, the 'cauterized conscience' that becomes 'senseless of sin, through sleeping in a careless security'.

In setting down his theory of political stability, James revealed his considerable experience of its alternatives – alternatives Shakespeare explores in *Macbeth*. Treason was a standard way of adjusting politics in Scotland, and James, who came to Scotland's throne as an infant, had survived several plots against him, including the latest, the Gowrie assassination plot of August 1600. His own father had been assassinated, and in 1587 he had watched from the sidelines as his mother, Mary, was executed by Queen Elizabeth for plotting to usurp her throne: like Macbeth, Mary was next-in-blood to the royal cousin whose kingdom she wanted, but, unlike Duncan, Elizabeth was no 'milksop'. In 1605 James again was targeted by terrorists: Londoners were agog at treason discovered right in their midst, the Gunpowder Plot, a pro-Catholic conspiracy led by Guy Fawkes that aimed to blow up Parliament and the King when he arrived for the state opening on 5 November. In March they followed the arraignment and trial of the plotters (as the King did, too, attending the hearings privately, incognito). Among the conspirators was the Jesuit Henry Garnet, who in his defence notoriously espoused the doctrine of 'equivocation', that, under oath, one could swear a lie and still keep conscience – but Garnet was executed anyway. (His doctrine is voiced in *Macbeth* where Shakespeare's equivocating Porter plays stand-up comic opposite Macbeth's straight-man equivocator.)

James was also interested in witchcraft. *Demonology* (1597) was his retort to Reginald Scot's widely read and heavily sceptical *Discovery of Witchcraft* (1584), in which Scot 'discovered' witchcraft to be fraudulent and accusers 'crying witch' merely malicious. James's sensational tract countered by setting a scene of 'the fearful abounding at this time in this country of these detestable slaves of the Devil, the Witches'. For James in 1597, witchcraft was real – and present. Some years earlier he had personally examined Agnes Sampson, the record of whose witchcraft trial circulated in England in a pamphlet titled *News from Scotland* (1591) – a pamphlet, it seems likely, that Shakespeare read. Players in that drama included one David Seaton, one 'Geillis Duncane', and someone identified only as 'the Porter's wife of Seaton' – names that coincidentally later turn up in *Macbeth*. When James dismissed some of Sampson's 'miraculous and strange' confession as 'extreme' lies, she took him aside and 'declared unto him the very words which passed' between himself 'and his Queen at Oslo in Norway the first night of their marriage', words, said the King, 'that all the Devils in hell could not have discovered'. In London in 1603 he ordered the reprinting of his *Demonology* and sponsored Parliament's re-enactment of a (toughened-up) statute on witchcraft – which he never caused to be repealed even though, as years went by, he grew sceptical on the subject and spent more time exposing false charges and quashing convictions than discovering witches.

James had one further 'interest' relevant to *Macbeth*. Like Shakespeare's Thane of Fife, James 'had a wife' (V.1.41), Anna of Denmark, a woman of no small political intelligence whose mere presence shifted the power dynamic of the monarchy. For the first time since Elizabeth I's accession in 1558, the Queen of England was not a sovereign but a consort, not the voice of power but the prompting word in power's ear, and not a virgin but an abundant breeder: between 1594, when her first child, Prince Henry, was born, and 1606 she sustained eight pregnancies; only three of her children survived infancy. Anna was fiercely, even, paradoxically, murderously maternal, one who quite possibly might have 'dashed' her baby's 'brains out', as Lady Macbeth threatens, to prove a point (I.7.58). As it was, she did something equally staggering. The custom in Scotland was to remove royal babies from their mother into the hands of official guardians, a practice utterly unnatural and shocking to Danish Anna. Wild with grief when her baby Henry was taken from her and determined to win back custody, she appealed first to her husband. James upheld custom. So Anna travelled to the residence where Henry stayed, stood in the stone courtyard and beat herself in the stomach until she aborted the child she was then carrying. James changed his mind and Henry was handed over. But his 'wayward' Queen continued to prove difficult. In London, on Twelfth Night 1605, she shocked the English court when she and her ladies blacked up to play the daughters of Niger in the first great masque of the new reign, devised by Anna herself, *The Masque of Blackness*. Shakespeare's *Othello* had played at court two months earlier (did his Moor prompt her daughters of Niger?), and he perhaps remembered the black-faced Queen when, not long after, in a play containing a clear

homage to James in the role of Augustus Caesar, he
wrote a stunning part for a 'wrangling' black Queen
of Egypt, Cleopatra. This traffic of performance memories might at least suggest that if James figured in
Shakespeare's 'Scottish play', Anna did too. It was not
forgotten that her first entrance into Scottish history was
tainted by witches: she was the young bride being carried
in the wedding flotilla that was wrecked, supposedly by
witch-raised storms on the North Sea, as it tried to reach
Scotland in 1589.

Citing these histories I am not proposing to read
Macbeth as a topical play so much as remembering that
Shakespeare's plays, whenever they are set, are saturated
with the materials of his present, always in conversation
with immediate events: eleventh-century Scotland 'knows'
Jacobean London. And that original sense of temporal
doubleness embedded in the plays persists: when we look
at a Shakespeare play today it strikes us as leading a double
life. It belongs to the early modern past but also to our
postmodern present. Its performance is both a revival
and a premiere. Another way to think about it is to see
every Shakespeare play as a set of parallel texts. One of
them is an object, the other an organism. The object is
the play-text, whose first version was the playhouse manuscript called the 'book'. It comprises the words of the
play, words that originated in early modern England and
that have been handed down to us in various printed
copies – quartos and folios – used by editors to compile
our modern editions. Because it is an object, we can
examine and appreciate this first kind of text like an arte-
fact, like, say, an Etruscan vase. But in the case of a play-
text, the 'book' is also a script, and the peculiar thing
about a script is that it is a radically incomplete text. It
contains instructions towards something that is never

written down, the performance – that is, the action, characterization, gestures, visual effects, costumes, sound: everything that turns the words into *play*, and not just the 'original' performance of *Macbeth* but all the subsequent performances the *Macbeth* play-text has been turned to in its 400-year afterlife in the theatre. Let's call this second, unrecorded but live and *experienced* text the 'performance text' to distinguish it from the comparatively fixed 'play-text'. In performance, *Macbeth* always exceeds the words printed in any edition of the play. Take, for example, that word 'Macbeth'. Simply by casting one actor or another in the central role – Ian McKellen vs. Antony Sher vs. Jon Finch vs. James Frain – *Macbeth* changes. Putting Macbeth in doublet and hose, black leather, commando gear or blue jeans alters how spectators understand the role and the world the role inhabits. So does setting the play in a medieval castle or on an inner-city housing estate. If the play-text is relatively closed, the performance text is wide open and hospitable to any number of interpretations, which means that *Macbeth* has been accruing layers of new meaning since its first performance, every time it engages with new actors and new audiences in new theatres in new generations.

As it happens the earliest text we have for *Macbeth*, the version printed in the 1623 first Folio, shows this organic process already at work: traces of subsequent performances are actually inscribed on its textual surface and they show other hands at work on *Macbeth* than Shakespeare's. Which is also to say that there are things printed in this text that Shakespeare did not write: all of Act III, scene 5 (the Hecat scene) and, in Act IV, scene 1, lines 39–43 and 124–31 (Hecat's return with a chorus-line of witches performing song-and-dance routines).

The early-twentieth-century director Harley Granville Barker described this material as 'True twaddle' – and knew it was not by Shakespeare, for Shakespeare, he pronounced firmly, 'was not in a twaddling mood when he wrote *Macbeth*'. The interpolations are probably Thomas Middleton's, the giveaway, the 'cue for a song' that marks each addition, '*Come away, come away, &c.*' at III.5.35 and '*Black Spirits, &c.*' at IV.1.43. These are the first lines of songs that appear in full in Middleton's *The Witch*, a play, like *Macbeth*, owned and performed by the King's Men. But why were Middleton's songs marked for insertion in *Macbeth* – and when? Simon Forman, the astrologer-cum-quack, saw *Macbeth* at the Globe in April 1611 and left an eye-witness account – not a bad synopsis for a first-time spectator, even given that his viewing was evidently contaminated by his reading: he calls the Weird Sisters 'fairies or Nymphs', straight out of Holinshed. What stuck in Forman's mind were *Macbeth*'s shocks and 'starts': the 'all hails', the prodigies attending the murder, the ghost, the wrecked feast, the sleepwalking, and 'the blood on [Macbeth's] hands that could not be washed off by any means'. But Forman makes no mention of Hecat – or her sensational 'production numbers'. Does his silence suggest that she was not in *Macbeth* in 1611? So when did she arrive?

Answering that question would be easier if we could date Middleton's *The Witch*. We can't – but we know it alludes to the most notorious scandal ever dragged through the Jacobean court, the Howard–Devereux divorce case of 1613. She, Frances Howard, Lady Essex, wanted the divorce so she could marry Robert Carr, the King's favourite. He, Robert Devereux, the hapless Earl of Essex, was inclined to let her go, but reneged when it emerged that she had consulted a 'wise woman' – a witch – to 'make away her Lord'. As the case lurched on – the King impatient for closure, the bishops weighing-in and bogging things down – Essex assented, but refused to admit to the only admissible (and wholly fabricated) grounds for an annulment, sexual 'insufficiency', because that would debar him from remarrying – which would leave him childless, his earldom without an heir. His lawyers settled upon equivocation: he would 'confess his insufficiency' towards Frances but would insist that he was '*maleficiatus* only *ad illam*': that is, impotent by witch-craft, but only towards her.

It is this farcical scenario, hot gossip in London in April 1613, that Middleton scripted in one of the plots in *The Witch* where Antonio, the husband, is impotent with his wife but shows no 'insufficiency' in bed with his doxy, his strumpet, and where Hecat and her crew are serio-comic hocus-pocus merchants responsible for his marital indisposition. They are thoroughly menacing, with their traffic in carcasses of bastard babies, but they also stage an operatic witches' Sabbath, complete with echo-songs and a flying cat.

The Essexes were divorced in October 1613; at Christmas that year Frances was married as if for the first time, 'in her hair' – that is, as a virgin – to Carr, newly created Earl of Somerset. The King reportedly bestowed £10,000 in jewels on the bride, and Thomas Middleton wrote a wedding masque for the occasion. But eighteen months later the golden couple crashed. Rumours started circulating about the death of Sir Thomas Overbury, Somerset's high-flying secretary who had loudly opposed the divorce, conveniently dying just days before it was finalized: a nasty death, said at the time to be caused by syphilis. Now it was claimed he had been poisoned. The Somersets were arrested for Overbury's murder in

October 1615, arraigned the following April and came to trial thoroughly implicated by the rout of small-time accomplices who had already gone to the gallows. Anne Turner, Frances's servant and intimate (unkind contemporaries called Frances a witch and Anne her 'familiar'), confessed that years earlier they had consulted Simon Forman about the annulment and used spells and wax effigies to advance it. (Forman could not be summoned; he had died in 1612.) 'Thus much for witchcraft,' the prosecutor commented. 'Now for poisoning.' Turner and Frances both confessed, but Carr protested his innocence. All were convicted, but only Turner was executed. The tarnished couple spent the next six years in the Tower.

What does this mean for *Macbeth*? If Middleton's *The Witch* was written and staged as a satire in the months following the sex-scandal divorce when '*maleficiatus ad illam*' was a smutty joke and everyone in the theatre knew who the gormless husband, the delightful 'Francisca' and the comic Scot really were, after the arraignments the case was altered. Now witchcraft was no laughing matter, and neither was murder. *The Witch*, I suggest, was removed from the repertoire because events had made its comedy dangerous. But the King's Men had another witch play in stock, one tuned to the fearful, imagination-stunned times and one able to capitalize on the suddenly massive popular interest in witchcraft. It may be that as the trial of Frances Howard proceeded and she was cast more luridly in the role of 'fiendlike' spouse and 'whore, wife, widow, witch' in the broadside ballads while Carr was represented by contemporaries as merely misled – 'if he had not met with such a woman he might have been a good man' – Shakespeare's company revived *Macbeth*. If they keyed his now ten-year-old tragedy to current events by importing from Middleton scenes that would trigger a cross-reference and pull the absent comedy into play, they also used those scenes to extend *Macbeth* just where sensation-seeking spectators would want more, adding witch material that, relocated, darkened Middleton's spectacles, overwriting them with a new power to disturb. By this time, late April 1616, Shakespeare was dead; any additions to *Macbeth* would have to be made by somebody else.

As I see it the 'other author'-marked Folio text of *Macbeth* is not 'corrupt' or a 'problem'; rather, it offers us an opportunity. It shows us a working script bearing traces of its ongoing life in the playhouse, where the 'book' belonged to the players who treated it to the same updating as was performed upon, say, Christopher Marlowe's *Doctor Faustus* or Thomas Kyd's *Spanish Tragedy*. At a time when most plays vanished from the active repertoire in a matter of weeks, those two crowd-pleasing tragedies of the late 1580s were still being performed a decade, even two decades, later. Reviving them, the players commissioned revisions: in 1602 William Bird and Samuel Rowley rewrote the comic parallel plot in *Faustus*, updating the jokes; in 1601 Ben Jonson added material that elaborated the mad scenes in Kyd. Like those additions, Middleton's interpolations in *Macbeth* can be read as a contemporary gloss on the play, particularly the black joke Hecat shares with her cronies, 'you all know security | Is mortals' chiefest enemy' (III.5.32–3). Even more significantly, Middleton's additions determined the play's afterlife in the theatre. At the Restoration, when William Davenant revived *Macbeth*, it was Middleton's version he adapted into the operatic spectacle that Samuel Pepys in 1667 thought was 'one of the best plays for . . . variety of dancing and music, that ever I saw', a show our theatre today would undoubtedly bill *Macbeth: The Musical*. Davenant's witches not only sang and danced; they flew – and even more unbelievably, they *survived*. The *Macbeth* Davenant derived from Middleton remained standard in the theatre until the 1850s. Over the years Hecat's crew expanded into a fifty-strong *corps de ballet mauvais* performing, as the name suggests, ugly dancing, a hags' ball. Clearly, subsequent performances of *Macbeth* were more and more fascinated by the play's 'instruments of darkness' (I.3.123) – a fascination that bears thinking about.

FIRST THINGS/'FIRSTLINGS'

Holinshed starts his *Chronicle* history of Macbeth with genealogies. Shakespeare starts with witches:

Thunder and Lightning. Enter three Witches. (Folio stage direction)

Shakespeare starts, that is, with trouble:

1. When shall we three meet againe?
   In Thunder, Lightning, or in Raine?
2. When the Hurley-burley's done,
   When the Battaile's lost, and wonne.
3. That will be ere the set of Sunne.
1. Where the place?
2. Upon the Heath.
3. There to meet with *Macbeth*.
1. I come, *Gray-Malkin*.
All. Padock calls anon: faire is foule, and foule is faire,
   Houer through the fogge and filthie ayre.   *Exeunt.*

And then they're gone.
   Transcribed exactly from the Folio to reproduce the

earliest textual evidence we have of the playwright's instructions towards performance (or lack of them), this opening scene demonstrates Shakespeare's habitual practices in using first scenes to lay down imagery like mines, set to detonate across the rest of the play. He establishes an acoustic or speech rhythm and a specific vocabulary for the play, but also a rhetoric, a *way* of speaking. And he introduces a visual field, a material apparatus the performance will employ and inhabit. In *Macbeth* he packs all this into just ten lines, a lightning bolt of an opening scene that strikes and vanishes before spectators can do much more than 'start', as Macbeth will later do. This scene is an induction into strangeness that anticipates Macbeth's first encounter with 'strange intelligence' (I.3.75). What it later does to him it first does to the audience. It offers us a preliminary case study in doubt.

Everything about this little scene troubles interpretation. It sounds strange. The 'standard acoustic' on Shakespeare's stage is the iambic pentameter – 'de *dum*, de *dum*, de *dum*, de *dum*, de *dum*' – like Macbeth's first line in the play, 'So foul and fair a day I have not seen' (I.3.37). By contrast, 'When shall we three meet again? | In thunder, lightning, or in rain?' gives us a lopped line, a reversed stress – '*dum* dum, *dum* dum, *dum* dum, *dum*' – like an arrhythmic heartbeat or the approach sound of the shark in Steven Spielberg's classic movie, *Jaws*, that sends our pulse into tachycardiac overdrive. There is something bizarre about the rhyme structure: again / rain, done / won. It is as though the questions posed ('When?', 'Where?') are not open but closed, locked in to predestined answers, rhyme itself a kind of prophetic voice: won / sun, heath / Macbeth. And then there is the rhetoric of the scene. The play opens with a question – '*When* shall we three meet again?' And the next three scenes do, too: 'What bloody man is that?', 'Where hast thou been, sister?', 'Is execution done on Cawdor?' These questions produce the uncanny sense of a play-world deeply doubting itself, in need of answers that frequently fail to arrive, but at the same time, paradoxically, a play-world in which the future is already fixed, all the answers known. Almost every line of this opening contains a further question, a paradox or antithesis, an ambiguity or double meaning: 'When the battle's lost and won', 'Fair is foul, and foul is fair.' This is the rhetoric of equivocation, of double talk, and it turns out to be the characteristic idiom of this play. As L. C. Knights has memorably observed of lines like these, with their 'sickening see-saw rhythm' ('Cannot be ill, cannot be good', I.3.130), the rhetoric of *Macbeth* suggests 'the kind of metaphysical pitch-and-toss that is about to be played with good and evil'. The moral equations such lines propose are terrifying. If 'the battle's lost and won', does that mean that winning and losing are going to be somehow the *same* in *Macbeth*? And if 'fair is foul and foul is fair', how do you discriminate? How do you recognize damnation or grace? How do you know who you're looking at?

The opening scene finds that last question particularly troubling. (And it will continue to vex: Duncan, at I.4.12–15, will say of the subject he never expected to betray him, 'He was a gentleman on whom I built | An absolute trust.' But you just can't tell. For 'There's no art | To find the mind's construction in the face'.) Using all our 'art' in Act I, scene I, what do we make of 'we three'? Later, Banquo will describe them as creatures of antithesis and paradox: 'Live you? Or are you . . . ?', 'You should be women; | And yet . . .' (I.3.41, 44–5). He calls them 'fantastical' – that is, phantom creations of his imagination (52). Yet 'outwardly' they 'show', they are corporeal (53). But then they '*vanish*', like bubbles in water or 'breath into the wind' (78, 81). In Act I, scene 1 the text does not give us much help deciding who or what 'we three' are. They do not name each other or themselves. The Folio speech-prefixes make them '1.', '2.', '3.'. Only in the stage directions are they '*Witches*' – and only once in performance, stunningly, at I.3.6, when the 'rump-fed ronyon' seems to know exactly to whom she is refusing a share of her chestnuts – 'Aroint thee, witch!' she cries. She may be right. For the 'witch' herself reports the taunt – without denying it. In that later scene 'we three' call themselves 'The weyward [that is, weird] Sisters', and 'Weird Sisters' is the name Macbeth knows when he cites them in his letter to his wife at I.5.7, and Banquo remembers when he admits dreaming about them in Act II, scene 1. But what is a 'witch'? Or a 'weird sister'?

In Act I, scene 1 we do not know. (Remember: we don't hear the word 'witch' in this play until I.3.6.) And if the text doesn't tell us, neither does performance: Banquo's flummoxed comments in Act I, scene 3, as we have seen, only get the measure of the Weird Sisters by finding them incomprehensible. They are enigmas, bodied (they 'show') but not bodied (they 'vanish') – which exposes the confusions between the material and the supernatural that make the Weird Sisters' agency in the play so problematic. What we *do* know in Act I, scene 1 is that they are coming back, and they have already identified a future they call 'Macbeth'. When we reflect upon it later, we will not be able to cite a time in this play *before* the witches, *before* their interference – or contamination. (Compare *Hamlet* or *A Midsummer Night's Dream*, plays that start with scenes of routine life – sentry duty, wedding preparations, a family row – before encounters with a ghost or with fairies turn their play-worlds upside down.)

It is instructive at this point to remember King James and his user's guide to witchcraft, *Demonology*. His book tells us things we need to know – things, certainly, that Shakespeare's *Macbeth* needs to know – about the 'instruments of darkness'. For one thing, they work 'by God's permission'. In a universe where God is omnipotent and omniscient, how could it be otherwise? And yet, considering the implications *for man*, it is a staggering thought, that God *allows* Satan free scope to work upon Macbeth. On the other hand (and this is meant to *comfort* us), 'God will not permit' Satan 'to deceive his own: but only such, as first wilfully deceives themselves'. So is that Macbeth? A willing self-deceiver? Or, more worryingly, is he the allowed victim of Satan because he was never 'his' – that is, God's – 'own', never one of the elect chosen for salvation but someone always scheduled for damnation? On the question of prophecy and whether the devil and his servant-witches know man's future, *Demonology* cavils. Only God is prescient. But because the devil is 'worldly wise' he can judge the 'likelihood of things to come' by what 'hath passed before'. So witches know our future not because they're seers but 'see-ers' who've kept surveillance on our past. They've been watching us. They're our 'familiars'! No wonder then, that, unknown to him, the Weird Sisters know Macbeth. As *Demonology* understands it, the power witches have to raise apparitions is linked to Satan's role as 'the father of all lies'. Satan is 'God's Ape', merely a counterfeiter fashioning crude simulacra of God's true creations. It follows that his agents are 'Ape's apes', and their apparitions are fakes. Still, these fakers can make mischief that feels real. They can raise storms, kill your cattle, unsex you, make you insomniac, cross the sea in a sieve: all of these are witch claims reported in *News from Scotland* and repeated in *Macbeth*. But the power permitted witches is limited – as the story of the 'master o'the *Tiger*' in Act I, scene 3 shows. He has gone to Aleppo, but he is not out of harm's way, for, says First Witch,

> . . . in a sieve I'll thither sail
> And like a rat without a tail
> I'll do, I'll do, and I'll do.

She promises a hell of pain. But though he 'shall be tempest-tossed', still his 'bark cannot be lost' (8–10, 24–5).

Paradoxically, the instruction we take from King James makes *Demonology*'s witches as ambiguous as *Macbeth*'s: both laughably impotent (on God's stage, Satan is never going to play anything but the bit-part Porter) and terrifyingly powerful (it dawns on us that our part, as mortals, is perpetually to crew the *Tiger*). But can we take their power seriously? Sailing in a sieve is a trick on a par with Dr Faustus's party pieces staged to entertain his big-shot patrons, but hardly the sort of crime against natural law that will topple order into universal uproar (even though, iconographically, the sieve is the emblem of chastity and its appropriation by witches is monstrous). But what if we rethought the witches' power under a different name, replacing their impudent 'sieve' with the synonym that appears alongside it in the witchcraft confession that so impressed King James – and Shakespeare, who, it seems clear, read *News from Scotland* in print? Agnes Sampson told the King that witches 'went by sea each one in a riddle or sieve'. These implements are the same. Sieves

sift fine grains, riddles, coarse ones, like gravel or cinders
(or on Judgement Day, calloused souls, calcified con-
sciences). With its big holes, which guarantee instant
sinking, a riddle makes an even more mystifying vessel
than a sieve. Of course, a riddle is that other thing too
– a verbal puzzle that equivocates, a kind of magic
performed with utterance, simultaneously transparent and
opaque, begging interpretation and blocking it. A floating
riddle then – is a riddle. Which is just the sort of joke
Macbeth enjoys: what sets Shakespeare's witches apart
from King James's is a sense of humour addicted to word
games.

Let us suppose, for wit's sake, that Shakespeare's
witches appreciate the pun and 'travel' in the second sort
of riddle. That might suggest that their real power to
disturb systems resides in their ability to *speak* riddles.
The temptation they offer, then, is not their 'supernatural soliciting', their 'prophetic greeting', but their
'imperfect' – that is, incomplete – speaking. They talk
in riddles that Macbeth is prompted to complete – to
'make perfect' – by filling in the blanks to work out the
doubtful, uncertain terms. That is what he is doing when
he first responds to the Weird Sisters' 'All hails'. 'By
Sinell's death,' he says, 'I know I am Thane of Glamis.'
But then, perplexed, he asks, 'how of Cawdor? The Thane
of Cawdor lives' (I.3.70–71). That is, Macbeth hears
'Cawdor' as a riddle. How, he is demanding, can *I* be
Cawdor when *someone else* is Cawdor? The point is that
Macbeth is perplexed by the wrong word. The riddle
word isn't 'Cawdor' but 'lives'. For as Macbeth learns
from Angus thirty-seven lines later in the kind of classic
utterance this play delivers without even batting an eye,
making verbs agents of metaphysical duplicity, Cawdor
is both riddlingly alive – and dead: 'Who was the Thane

lives yet' (108). How balefully this new echo falls upon our ears! That Cawdor 'bears that life' that 'he deserves to lose' (109–10) makes him 'lost and won', an irony intensified by the onstage action where even now Macbeth is slipping on the not-yet-vacated title, pre-empting Cawdor as he will King Duncan.

When a seemingly plain and familiar word like 'lives' grows doubtful, it is time to doubt the operation of all utterance. Soon enough in *Macbeth* we will observe a wayward migration of language, words starting in the Weird Sisters' mouths later rolling off other people's tongues. 'Fair is foul' returns as Macbeth's entry line, 'So foul and fair a day I have not seen' (I.3.37); 'lost and won' echoes in Duncan's exit line: 'What he hath lost, noble Macbeth hath won' (I.2.70). We will observe how plain-talking words knot into riddles – like the opening word of the play. And we will see how, from these first things, *Macbeth* never recovers.

'WHEN?'/'NOW'

The Weird Sisters tell Macbeth he will be king. And they 'refer' him 'to the coming on of time' (I.5.7–8). But they don't say when. And 'when' is the only thing that matters.

Their prediction violates time, as prediction literally must, by collapsing the distance between the present and the future. The effect of that violation is to propose their predictions as riddles to be solved, and the energies they release drive Macbeth instantly from listening to action. He can't help it. It is the way the human mind works – for as Theseus observes (in *A Midsummer Night's Dream*, another play that tries to rationalize the irrational), man is endowed with imagination whose 'strong tricks' work like instant transmitters between brain and hand: 'if it would but apprehend some joy' it immediately 'comprehends some bringer of that joy' (V.1.19–20). No wonder, then, that hearing the predictions, Macbeth's imagination moves instantly from 'king' to 'assassination'. No wonder, either, that his immediate instinct is to stop time: 'Stay!' he cries (I.3.69).

Like *Othello*, a play framed by gossip and tale-telling – its first line is 'Tush, never tell me', its last word is 'relate' – *Macbeth* is similarly framed, by time-keeping and timing. 'When?' asks the First Witch at the very beginning. 'Now', answers Angus near the end (V.2.16, 18, 20). The play hangs poised between this question and its answer, which finally comes in Macduff's declaration 'The time is free' and Malcolm's closing promise that his restored monarchy 'will perform in measure, time, and place' (V.6.94, 112). In the interim Scotland watches clocks – or listens out for them. 'One: two: why then, 'tis time to do't,' whispers Lady Macbeth, cocking her ear to the phantom echoes in her head (V.1.34–5). 'Harpier cries! 'Tis time, 'tis time!' shrills the third Weird Sister at IV.1.3. In Act II, scene 1 Banquo and Fleance stand on the battlements scanning the empty heavens to know 'How goes the night' – but cannot tell. The moon is down, the star-candles 'out', the clock 'not heard' (1–2, 5). In Act I, scene 5 Lady Macbeth wonders of Duncan's unexpected arrival 'here tonight', 'And when goes hence?' Tomorrow? 'O never | Shall sun that morrow see!' (57–9). In Act II, scene 2 urgent knocks sound at the gate – it is Macduff, whom the King commanded 'to call timely on him' and he has 'almost slipped the hour'. (Indeed, he arrives too late.) Even so, the Porter dithers and dallies and jokes about growing 'old turning the key' – and delays opening (II.3.43–4, 2).

Every time an English speaker opens his mouth, he tells the time, for unlike, say, Chinese, English is a language whose verb tenses (from Latin *tempus*, time) locate our actions: present, past, future. They help us order our world. Listening to Macbeth react to the Weird Sisters' predictions we have the sickening sense of a mind losing its grasp on real time, getting lost in 'horrible imaginings'. His soliloquy at I.3.126–41 is structured by time markers, but his verbs slip and slide as if he is staggering through a drunkard's dream: 'Two truths are told', he begins, wonderingly, of the predictions. Of the three, two have already come true! How rapidly is the future becoming the past! These 'happy prologues' give 'me earnest of [future] success' by 'Commencing [now] in a truth': 'I am [now, present tense] Thane of Cawdor.' But then Macbeth is catapulted into a future of 'horrible imaginings' and 'fantastical . . . surmise' that operate real effects upon his body *now*: the 'image' of an assassination that has not happened 'yet' makes his hair stand on end, his 'seated heart knock at [his] ribs'. He tries to hold the future at bay: 'If chance will . . . chance may' (143). And further distances it – 'Come what come may' (146) – before consigning it to the past: 'My dull brain was wrought | With things forgotten' (149–50). But are they? His final speech to Banquo already remembers 'things forgotten' *in the future*:

> Think upon what hath chanced, and at more time,
> The interim having weighed it, let us speak
> Our free hearts each to other . . .
> Till then, enough! (153–6)

Significantly, when Macbeth contemplates the murder of Duncan he is not thinking about power, politics or

ambition, but about time, agonizing over verbs, hypothesizing the relationship between 'do' and 'done':

> If it were done when 'tis done, then 'twere well
> It were done quickly. If the assassination
> Could trammel up the consequence, and catch
> With his surcease success – that but this blow
> Might be the be-all and the end-all! (I.7.1–5)

If, he argues, a murder is completed when it is performed,
you might as well do it – and be done with it. But maybe
it is not. Maybe 'this blow' is not the 'end-all'; maybe it
is just the beginning. Trying to fix the relationship
between 'when' and 'done', the present and the future,
Macbeth is really searching the relationship between the
temporal and the eternal, setting 'this bank and shoal of
[human] time' against 'the life to come' (6–7), that is,
salvation or damnation. Of course, there are other ways
of imagining the relationship between when and done.
Lady Macbeth, who sees no 'consequence' to her actions,
imagines 'what's done is done' (III.2.12). (Later, she
learns otherwise.) Like the Weird Sisters, she collapses
time, wanting the 'future in the instant' (I.5.56). For
them, however, the future happens in the continuous
present: 'I'll do, I'll do, and I'll do' (I.3.10).

Time in *Macbeth* accelerates. It takes Macbeth three
soliloquies and two conversations with his wife to work
up to Duncan's murder. He is significantly quicker with
Banquo; and the slaughter of Macduff's family is 'thought
and done', 'The very firstlings of my heart' now 'The
firstlings of my hand' (IV.1.146–8). Enacting time's
acceleration, scenes shorten as the play goes on. Time
closes in. But paradoxically time also stops or replays
action as on a looped video tape. Day and night blur into

unrelieved darkness, Macbeth and his wife staggering through a limbo of sleeplessness where time is the nostalgic recollection of a past where the world worked according to known laws. In this new delirious world 'what's done' returns to 'do, do and do' again. The dead return. Almost comically aggrieved by Banquo's pushy ghost, Macbeth remembers 'The times has been' that when you beat a man's brains out 'the man would die, | And there an end. But now they rise again . . . | And push us from our stools' (III.4.77–81).

But there are more terrible revenants than ghosts. There are the memories that haunt the mind. Staggering from the bloody chamber Macbeth trades questions with his wife that reveal minds unravelling:

MACBETH
  I have done the deed. Didst thou not hear a noise?
LADY
  I heard the owl-scream and the cricket's cry.
  Did not you speak?
MACBETH   When?
LADY   Now.
MACBETH   As I descended? (II.2.14–16)

Macbeth cannot stop retracing his steps: he replays the event, returning himself to the moments *before* it happened, remembering the groom who laughed in his sleep, the other who cried out, waking them both. He remembers hearing them both pray, saying 'Amen', an 'Amen' that stuck in his throat as he heard another voice crying, 'Sleep no more! | Macbeth does murder sleep' (35–6). Obsessively, Macbeth repeats 'sleep' eight times in the course of these and the next seven lines as his memory tape coils around his mind, his rising hysteria prompting hers. She insists that he must stop thinking: 'Consider it not so deeply', 'These deeds must not be thought | After these ways', 'You do unbend your noble strength, to think | So brain-sickly of things' (II.2.30, 33–4, 45–6). But the brain is a book where 'pains' are indelibly 'registered', 'where every day' one can 'turn | The leaf to read them' (I.3.150–52). And nothing, no medicine, rhubarb or senna, can 'Raze out the written troubles of the brain' (V.3.55, 42).

Spectators are offered an appalling look into one of these 'hurt minds' in Act V, scene 1. As Lady Macbeth walks in her sleep she literalizes the terrible metaphors that have been circulating in the text since the moment Macbeth 'murdered sleep' (II.2.42), enacting in her sleep-walking the past's return to capture the present. There is nothing to match this scene on the early modern stage, not even Ophelia's real and desperate madness that, played off against it, shames Hamlet's theatrically adolescent 'antic disposition'. Lady Macbeth lives out the terrible metaphors that Macbeth only imagines in his mind. Her 'eyes are open' but 'their sense are shut' (V.1.24–5) – exactly Macbeth's case! And while her body is present, her mind is elsewhere, stuck, remembering the past, re-enacting the murder night after night, counting the clock, smelling the blood, obsessed by 'a spot', bewildered by its profusion – 'who would have thought the old man to have had so much blood in him?' (38–9). Washing and washing the 'little hand' that 'All the perfumes of Arabia will not sweeten' (48–9), nothing she can do now will redeem the future. Indeed, her whole future belongs to this one action. This is what damnation looks like.

Registering true horror at his feigned 'discovery' of Duncan's body, Macbeth declared, 'Had I but died an

hour before this chance | I had lived a blessèd time'
(II.3.88–9). And he was right. For 'from this instant |
There's nothing serious in mortality' (89–90). Time *after*
the murder is meaningless. 'Tomorrow, and tomorrow,
and tomorrow' will produce only 'yesterdays' to light
'fools | The way to dusty death' (V.5.19, 22–3). Man is
no more than a 'poor player' (24), and his lifetime is as
inconsequential as the passage of fake stage time. It is a
tale 'Signifying nothing' (28). Nihilism in *Macbeth* is
nowhere bleaker than this emptying out of human time.

But by now the time-keeper has knocked at the gate
that has been opened by the one who calls himself the
'devil-porter' (II.3.16), rousing the household. And the
initial 'When?' of the Weird Sisters drops its delayed
response into place with Angus's account of Macbeth's
'now':

> Now does he feel
> His secret murders sticking on his hands;
> Now minutely revolts upbraid his faith-breach.
>   . . . Now does he feel his title
> Hang loose about him like a giant's robe
> Upon a dwarfish thief. (V.2.16–22)

Macbeth succeeds in killing a king, and killing sleep. But
he fails at his boldest attempt. He cannot kill time itself.
When he insisted that the Weird Sisters tell him whether
Banquo's children would reign in Scotland, they answered
with a '*show*', a line of kings that seemed that it might
'stretch out to the crack of doom', the end of time
(IV.1.116). The last one holds a mirror, and the mirror
multiplies the 'Horrible sight' (121) it frames. Is this
multiplication of the future the Weird Sisters' best joke?
Or their cruellest optical riddle?

'LIES LIKE TRUTH'

How do you know things? How do you test 'strange intelligence'? In *Othello* you demand 'ocular proof', the kind of proof you get when Desdemona enters and Othello knows by looking at her that Iago's pornographic fantasies are false:

> Desdemona comes:
> If she be false, O, then heaven mocks itself!
> I'll not believe't. (III.3.274–6)

In *Macbeth* this sort of knowing by looking is discredited (as it later fails in *Othello*), for as Duncan knows, 'There's no art | To find the mind's construction in the face' (I.4.12–13). The traitor's face is a 'vizard' to his thought (III.2.34); he is one who can 'look like the innocent flower, | But be the serpent under't' (I.5.63–4); who can 'mock the time with fairest show: | False face' hiding 'what the false heart doth know' (I.7.81–2). Young Malcolm in England, on the run from Macbeth's assassins, is an old-boy in the school of hypocritical two-facedness. Searching Macduff's face for tell-tale signs of treachery, he apologizes – but yet suspects:

> That which you are my thoughts cannot transpose;
> Angels are bright still though the brightest fell.
> Though all things foul would wear the brows of grace,
> Yet grace must still look so. (IV.3.21–4)

Even auspicious signs: how much do they signify? Look, says Banquo, scanning the bird's flight pattern above the battlements as the royal party stands on the threshold of Castle Inverness,

> This guest of summer,
> The temple-haunting martlet, does approve
> By his loved mansionry that the heaven's breath
> Smells wooingly here; no jutty, frieze,
> Buttress, nor coign of vantage, but this bird
> Hath made his pendent bed and procreant cradle;
> Where they most breed and haunt I have observed
> The air is delicate. (I.6.3–10)

Then his gaze turns to see a smiling Lady Macbeth enter to greet her royal guest.

If you're Hamlet, you test 'strange intelligence' – 'The spirit that I have seen | May be a devil . . . | I'll have grounds . . .' – by putting on a play so you can observe spectators' reactions and draw conclusions from your hypotheses: 'If a do blench', the Ghost is right, Claudius is a killer, and 'I know my course'. But 'If his occulted guilt | Do not itself unkennel', then Claudius is innocent and 'It is a damned ghost'. Either way, however, Hamlet resolves the problem of knowing: 'The play's the thing | Wherein I'll catch the conscience of the King' (II.2.596–601, 595, 596; III.2.90–92; II.2.602–3).

Hamlet's habits of hypothesizing are ones *Macbeth* picks up – though without the play as material 'grounds' to support Hamlet's conclusions. Writing on Shakespeare's histories – he is thinking specifically of the *Henry IV*s – John Kerrigan has wonderfully observed that these plays 'dilate into retrospection'. Just as certainly, the tragedies 'dilate' into hypothesis. But where retrospection is anchored in memory (even if the anchor of old men's memories drifts a bit), hypothesis in *Macbeth* free-wheels across the imaginary: 'If you can look into the seeds of time . . .'; 'If it were done when 'tis done . . .';

'If the assassination . . .'; 'If we should fail?'; 'If it be
so, | For Banquo's issue have I filed my mind'; 'If
charnel-houses . . . send | Those that we bury, back . . .';
'If thou speak'st false . . .'; 'If thy speech be sooth . . .'
(I.3.57; I.7.1, 2, 59; III.1.63–4; III.4.70–71; V.5.38, 40).
Unlike Hamlet's, Macbeth's hypotheses are not tested by
practice. They don't aim to 'know my course'. Instead,
they grope distractedly, clutching at metaphor. They
imagine things by imagining other things. In those lines
in Act I, scene 7 premeditating regicide – 'If the assassi-
nation | Could trammel up the consequence, and catch |
With his surcease success' – we observe how 'the assassination' is detached from the notional assassin. Macbeth's
hypothesis absents himself from the killing. Assassination
becomes the agent of its own doing, figuratively able to
cast a 'trammel' – a net – over 'consequence': this last
word is neatly neutral but loaded. In *Hamlet* we understand metaphorically how a play can 'catch' a 'conscience',
but how can a 'trammel' catch 'surcease'? And is 'success'
a species of 'surcease' – bagged in the same net? Or is it
what eludes 'consequence'?

Macbeth, A. R. Braunmuller has observed, is a play
that thinks through metaphor. At its simplest, metaphor
puts two things that the mind normally keeps separate
into a reciprocal rhetorical relationship, a little of each
rubbing off on the other. Metaphor works by poetic fric-
tion. In this play unearned titles are 'borrowed robes',
stolen ones 'Hang loose . . . like a giant's robe | Upon
a dwarfish thief'; a face is 'a book where men | May
read strange matters'; memory is planted with 'rooted
sorrow'; 'the sauce to meat is ceremony'; sleep is 'sore
labour's bath' (I.3.108; V.2.21–2; I.5.60–61; V.3.41;
III.4.35; II.2.38). More dangerously, though, metaphors
work euphemistically; they can legitimate the illegiti-

mate. If Malcolm, promoted heir-apparent, is 'a step', he can be 'o'erleap[ed]'; if Banquo is a 'snake', he can be 'scorched'; if Macduff's boy is an 'egg', he can be crushed (I.4.49–50; III.2.13; IV.2.83). Murder for Lady Macbeth is 'business' (I.5.66) – to be conducted. Such metaphors attempt to inoculate the understanding against the horrors they figure. 'The very firstlings of my heart shall be | The firstlings of my hand', resolves Macbeth (IV.1.146–7), a metaphor that explodes in our brains as the speech proceeds and we understand 'firstlings' to be not just first impulses but first-born children. 'I am in blood | Stepped in so far, that, should I wade no more, | Returning were as tedious as go o'er,' he observes (III.4.135–7), and our senses are so overwhelmed by what the metaphor figures, a vast sea of blood lapping the killer's thighs, that it takes some time for our intellects to kick in and unravel its logic. If 'wade no more' means 'end the killing', *why* is 'returning' like going 'o'er'? Will Macbeth have to slaughter his way back to the terra firma of innocence?

As people in this play try to understand the incomprehensible, their metaphors grow more strained, the ideas set against each other more violently incompatible. The search for analogy makes utterance restless. But more weirdly, it discovers that things can be known only by un-knowing them. Metaphor cancels the 'is-ness' of a thing, makes a thing radically *not* itself, as it proposes alternatives that take it further and further away from itself. Sleep is wool, water, medicine, food: it 'knits up the ravelled sleave of care'; it is 'sore labour's bath'; 'Balm of hurt minds'; 'nature's second course' (II.2.37–9). Life is 'a walking shadow'; 'a poor player'; 'a tale | Told by an idiot'; 'nothing' (V.5.24–8). Duncan murdered is an artwork, a 'masterpiece', but one made by 'Confusion'. He is a desecrated 'temple'; a sight-destroying Gorgon; 'The Great Doom's image' (II.3.63, 65, 68–9, 75). 'What do you mean?' cries Lady Macbeth at one point as her husband's utterance seems to go into spasm (II.2.40). We, too, can hardly make literal sense of speeches whose images congregate like insurgent ghost-armies mustering in hallucinations:

>   . . . his virtues
> Will plead like angels, trumpet-tongued against
> The deep damnation of his taking-off;
> And Pity, like a naked new-born babe
> Striding the blast, or heaven's cherubin, horsed
> Upon the sightless curriers of the air,
> Shall blow the horrid deed in every eye,
> That tears shall drown the wind. (I.7.18–25)

>   Come, seeling night,
> Scarf up the tender eye of pitiful day,
> And with thy bloody and invisible hand
> Cancel and tear to pieces that great bond
> Which keeps me pale. Light thickens
> And the crow makes wing to the rooky wood;
> Good things of day begin to droop and drowse,
> Whiles night's black agents to their preys do rouse.
>   (III.2.46–53)

Writing speeches like these it is as though Shakespeare was inventing a language to externalize the interior of Macbeth's mind, where reason, conscience, the imaginary and fantasy fight for words, where 'function is smothered in surmise' and 'nothing is but what is not' (I.3.140–41). And not just Macbeth's mind, for in this world metaphor seems to have a mind of its own. Think

about the switchbacks metaphor performs in these lines
on 'The merciless Macdonwald':

> Worthy to be a rebel, for to that
> The multiplying villainies of nature
> Do swarm upon him . . . (I.2.10–12)

The bloody Captain is saying that Macdonwald, as a
rebel, attracts to that master villainy every lesser villainy
in the world, isn't he? The question arises because the
metaphor, craftily, turns agent and victim around. It natu-
ralizes villainy – making villainy something nature
produces, a nest of bees or wasps or a seething anthill,
instead of a crime man commits. And then it turns these
'multiplying' hordes upon the criminal, making them
swarm horribly over the pestered rebel who becomes
the helpless, hapless victim. Or take Lady Macbeth,
summoning 'spirits | That tend on mortal thoughts' to
'unsex me here'. 'Come to my woman's breasts', she
urges. 'And take my milk for gall' (I.5.38–9, 45–6). Is she
ordering them to replace her milk with gall – or inviting
them to suckle her, saying her milk *is* gall? Again, Ross,
celebrating battlefield atrocities, tells Macbeth of his
astonishing feats: 'in the stout Norweyan ranks' you were
'Nothing afeard of what thyself didst make, | Strange
images of death' (I.3.94–6): but did Macbeth make those
'strange images' out of Norwegian bodies – or his own?

More than doubling back on itself, the language of
metaphor, like the riddling of the witches, shows a
tendency to migrate. Words uttered in one scene move
across to another where they pick up new meanings,
intensified, ironic, horrific. Things literal turn into
metaphors; metaphors become literal – like the 'air-drawn
dagger' of Macbeth's 'heat-oppressèd brain' that weirdly

materializes when, unable to clutch it, he draws his own weapon instead (III.4.61; II.1.39–41). Such strange transactions are typical. In Act II, scene 2 Macbeth kills a sleeping man, but registers that act as metaphor: 'Macbeth does murder sleep'. Murderers put on nightgowns, pretend to be sleepers, but indeed, 'Sleep no more' except 'In the affliction of these terrible dreams | That shake us nightly' (II.2.35; III.2.18–19). In Act V, scene 1 these metaphors culminate in the sleepwalking scene. '[P]ut on your nightgown', urges Lady Macbeth (58) – already wearing hers. As she walks and talks in that restless ecstasy that travesties sleep, the physician who is looking on is unable to apply the 'Balm of hurt minds' she nostalgically yearns for in her final words, 'To bed, to bed, to bed' (II.2.39; V.1.64).

The word 'banquet' – the common, everyday ritual of breaking bread, bonding family, clan, state through nurture – undergoes a similar journey during the course of the play. 'Banquet' first appears in the play as a metaphor. In Macbeth's 'commendations I am fed', says Duncan: 'It is a banquet to me' (I.4.56–7). Later, sleep is a banquet – 'Chief nourisher in life's feast' (II.2.40) – which Macbeth wastes when he kills sleeping Duncan. Thereafter he wastes his own coronation banquet (III.4). 'You know your own degrees,' he says, welcoming the Thanes who represent the order of his kingdom, 'sit down' (1). But over the next hundred lines he trashes the table, quailing terrified before the bloody ghost whom no one else can see but who arrives right on cue, fresh from the ditch where 'twenty trenchèd gashes' (26) should keep him down, but don't. Table, chairs, trenchers, thanes, wife, all these – the banquet's furniture – become shields to throw up between the trembling King and the sight that appals him. His thanes stand aghast; his wife tries to cover up; but the evidence of the wrecked banquet, the 'displaced . . . mirth' and 'admired disorder', is damning (108–9). As the thanes rush hugger-mugger for the exit we see the ruin of the kingdom in the banquet's debris. Left behind, the King and Queen sag wearily in the rubble, talking of this and that, wondering what time it is, yearning for sleep, knowing, even from the depths of their exhaustion, that there is so much more to do, that 'We are yet but young in deed' (143).

Of course, this wasn't the first banquet – nor the last. At the start of Act I, scene 7, as the Folio stage directions indicate, *'a Sewer'* – a chief waiter – *'and divers Servants with Dishes and Service'* pass *'over the Stage'*. They are carrying in to Duncan the banquet that celebrates Scotland's triumph – but Macbeth is absent, outside, chewing over possibility, 'If it were done . . .' The activity of his mind is superimposed upon the actions of the Sewer that take place behind him: the dutiful servant sets off the murderous host, whose bloody thoughts make a mockery of the banquet happening next door. Even more of a mockery is the banquet that comes in Act IV, scene 1. The Weird Sisters crowd around the cauldron – 'Double, double, toil and trouble' – preparing a toxic mess of boiled body parts – entrails, eye, toe, tongue, leg, liver, nose, lips, and 'Finger of birth-strangled babe' (30) – that gets served up as apparitions *like* bodies to satisfy Macbeth's hunger for 'answer'. This is, metaphorically, his last supper – and he gets a belly full.

Watching scenes like these in performance we understand how a play makes us 'think sensuously' (Robin Grove's term) and 'see . . . feelingly' (Gloucester's in *King Lear*, IV.6.150). 'Will all great Neptune's ocean wash this blood | Clean from my hand?' wonders Macbeth staring, horrified, at hands that, spongy with Duncan's blood, look flayed (II.2.60–61). We *know* it is Duncan's blood – yet it appears to us that Macbeth is the one bleeding to death, all the nerve endings on his raw hands exposed to pain. Brightly his wife assures him that 'A little water clears us of this deed' (67), and holds up hands stained like his. But Duncan's blood is even now draining into the fabric of her being. Its taint will not be cleared by any amount of water. For the 'spot' the sleep-walker will rub, night after night, washing her hands, finding it on her skin, will have seeped into the brain.

Participating in such scenes of anguish, spectators learn an even harder lesson than pain from metaphor in *Macbeth*. We learn that in a world which produces, indifferently, the 'ravined salt sea shark' and the 'temple-haunting martlet' (IV.1.24; I.6.4), a world where equiv-ocation is not abnormal but lies 'at the heart of things' (again, as Robin Grove puts it), in this world equivoca-tion is going to be constitutive of language, too. Simply, all language is metaphor. At best, it's an approximation that tries to match what we *think* to what we *say*. All language performs a kind of 'juggling' act, and all words, at some level, 'palter with us in a double sense' (V.6.58, 59). Like 'the equivocation of the fiend', language, even at the best of times, 'lies like truth' (V.5.43–4).

While Shakespeare was writing *Macbeth*, he was reading John Florio's English translation of the essays of Michel de Montaigne, and no doubt came across the essay 'Of Liars'. In it Montaigne reproves lying as the most 'detestable vice' man is capable of. 'Nothing makes us men,' he writes, 'and no other means keeps us bound to one another but our word.' Lying violates our word, the only maker of the social contract. And as it baffles, lying multiplies confusion that works ultimately to the collapse of government, order, culture. We have little defence against the liar: 'If a lie had no more faces but one, as truth hath, we should be in far better terms than we are. For whatsoever a liar should say, we would take it in a contrary sense. But the opposite of a truth hath many many shapes, and an indefinite field.'

'Nothing makes us men . . . but our word': and that makes us easy targets. Not least because 'truth' and 'lie' are not so distinct as Montaigne proposes. We humans do not just speak truths or lies; we tell jokes, we quibble, use puns and double entendres, we speak riddles 'That keep the word of promise to our ear' but 'break it to our hope' (V.6.60–61). Are these speech acts lies – or ways of telling the truth? In the end Macbeth is destroyed, but not by some extraordinary intervention of the supernatural. He is destroyed by that thing that makes us 'men': words. Facing Macduff, invulnerable, as he thinks –

> I bear a charmèd life which must not yield
> To one of woman born –

Macbeth finally learns how language works in this play. 'Despair thy charm,' Macduff answers,

> And let the angel whom thou still hast served
> Tell thee Macduff was from his mother's womb
> Untimely ripped. (V.6.51–5)

Ah! Like puzzling over 'Cawdor' (all that long time ago) when the trick word was 'lives', Macbeth has staked his future on 'woman'. But the word that 'lies like truth' is 'born'.

'SEEDS OF TIME'

When Ross arrives in England, carrying news to the exiles, his view of Scotland is apocalyptic:

>   Alas, poor country,
> Almost afraid to know itself! It cannot
> Be called our mother, but our grave . . . (IV.3.164–6)

Describing Macbeth's subjects as Scotland's children touches a terrible truth. Macbeth's totalitarianism is a war against the future and, ultimately, against children. In a play that sups 'full with horrors' (V.5.13), none exceeds the horrors imagined through and performed upon the bodies of children.

Singling out the child as 'perhaps the most powerful symbol in the tragedy', Cleanth Brooks showed how deeply 'childness' is rooted in *Macbeth*. Children appear as characters (Banquo's Fleance, Macduff's 'Young fry' (IV.2.84), the 'lily-livered boy' who, white-faced, reports the approach of the 10,000-strong English army at V.3.15). They are symbols in material form (the '*Bloody Child*' and '*Child Crowned*' that rise as apparitions (IV.1.75, 85)). They figure within metaphors ('Pity' is 'like a naked new-born babe | Striding the blast'; 'duties' to Duncan's 'throne and state' are 'children and servants' while murderous inspirations are 'firstlings' and 'noble passion' is integrity's 'Child'). The image of the child draws together the play's stake in history, both its ambitions for 'Tomorrow, and tomorrow, and tomorrow' and its nostalgia for a 'blessèd' yesterday, a time of grace before memory came to figure as wasteground rooted only with sorrow. From the Weird Sisters' initial 'When?', *Macbeth* is concerned with futures – prophetic, dynastic, domestic, metaphysical, eternal – and the child is their material embodiment. But the child also represents a longing for the adult's past: when he, too, was innocent and his mind uncontaminated by those 'cursèd thoughts' (II.1.8) that even good men like Banquo brood upon. It is an irony, of course, that Macbeth wants both to possess the future – the one the Weird Sisters 'gave' him – and to destroy it – the one they 'promised' Banquo. It follows that Macbeth's war against the future is a war on children.

What about his own parental status? Lady Macbeth claims to have 'given suck' and to know 'How tender 'tis to love the babe that milks me' (I.7.54–5). But Macbeth's meditation at III.1.60–71 and Macduff's desolate cry at IV.3.215 make clear 'He has no children'. This discrepancy may mean much – or nothing. In the theatre, however, it cannot be ducked: every actor who plays Lady Macbeth must interpret 'I have given suck', and every actor who plays her husband must interpret what he hears. It is possible, of course, that Lady Macbeth's line is one of those utterances among many in this play that 'palter with us in a double sense' (V.6.59). Whatever its status as 'real history', however, its urgent force in Act I, scene 7 is rhetorical and performative.

Her line comes at the end of a pair of speeches whose objective is to make a man of Macbeth. He has decided against the murder: 'We will proceed no further in this business' (I.7.31). She counters with questions – 'Was the hope drunk . . . ? Hath it slept . . . ?' (35–6). Her nagging sours hope into a drunkard's dream and reduces the crown to an accessory Macbeth wants but fears to catch even when it is thrown into his lap. She makes him a cat, a beast, a sot sick on ambition's fantasies. But a man? She only constructs him as a man in one of those hypothetical past-futures this play is constantly imagining: 'When you durst do it, then you were a man' (I.7.49). And it is as she is juggling these terms – 'make', 'unmake', 'more', 'much more' – that she slips in her stunning non sequitur, 'the babe that milks me', using the remembered child to set up, through a syntax of conditionals, a terrifying image of what *she* would do to get the crown:

> I would while it was smiling in my face
> Have plucked my nipple from his boneless gums
> And dashed the brains out, had I so sworn as you
> Have done to this. (56–9)

To make a man of Macbeth, Lady Macbeth produces the death of the child.

And his limp response? 'Bring forth men-children only!' (72). But the only children brought forth to Macbeth are the monster babies, part restorations of a 'birth-strangled babe', that surface in the witches' cauldron.

It is worth noticing that while the child of destiny, Fleance, escapes in the dark, the child who is killed as his proxy, Macduff's little 'egg', suffers in the light. His murder is the one killing in *Macbeth* that the playwright puts centre stage, in full view, requiring that spectators stare it straight in the face. It is worth noticing, too, that even as Macbeth sets himself up as a latter-day Herod, slaughtering all the infants so he will not be deposed, he knows his efforts are futile. The children will win. For like that babe called 'Pity' who, though naked and new born, is yet powerfully capable of riding out the storm Macbeth unleashes, the children of *Macbeth* are both midgets and giants, fragile eggs and mighty moving forests. They are the 'seeds of time' (I.3.57). And there is no way of keeping them down.

'DID HEAVEN LOOK ON'?

What do we take away from *Macbeth*? To the question
(if it needed asking) 'What are your chances of getting
away with murder?', the answer: Nil. Less straightfor-
wardly, reflections upon life's lottery, how the difference
between the sweetness of one man's life and the bitter-
ness of another's depends on accidents, chance encounters with strangers, opportunities offered that we grab
with both hands or toss aside or waste. There are no
'good guys' in *Macbeth*. Banquo has to beg the 'Merciful
powers' to 'Restrain in me the cursèd thoughts that
nature | Gives way to in repose' (II.1.7–9) because he
needs them restrained: he has been dreaming of witches
(20). Macduff confesses himself 'Sinful' (IV.3.223). He
knows it is his fault that his family died: 'Not for their
own demerits, but for mine, | Fell slaughter on their souls'
(225–6). (But what was his sin? His wife calls him a
traitor and thinks he fled. But isn't his demerit more like
culpable naivety, a failure of 'badness' – that he cannot
imagine his wife and children *are* in danger? No man,
not even a tyrant, kills *children*.) For his part, Malcolm
'proves' that he is an honest man by demonstrating that
he is an expert liar. So along with all his other 'king-
becoming graces' (91), Malcolm is equipped to play the
hypocrite. Then there is 'good' old Seyward, restoring
legitimate rule to Scotland – he and his 10,000 English
soldiers. We know from Holinshed that Seyward is
Malcolm's grandfather, which means he has 'some rights
of memory in this kingdom', as Fortinbras in *Hamlet*
might say (V.2.383). So is Seyward's army an army of
liberation – or of occupation, taking the first steps towards
annexing Scotland to the English crown? (In more 'true'

history, Malcolm's little brother, Donalbain, who disappeared to Ireland in Act II, returns to murder Malcolm's son. And Fleance, whom we last saw in Act III dodging Macbeth's thugs, flees to Wales where, taken into the King's household, he rapes his host's daughter, whereupon the King has him killed. It is the bastard son born of that rape who, growing to manhood as a steward in the royal household, produces Scotland's first Steward/Stewart/Stuart king.) In this catalogue of men, even Duncan is doubtful. If he has been so 'clear' in his 'great office' (I.7.18), why is he being attacked on three sides? Why is he responsible for 'another Golgotha' (I.2.41)? But if Duncan's goodness is doubtful, isn't Macbeth's *badness* doubtful, too? Macbeth still has the word 'hope' in his vocabulary in Act V (6.61).

Given the danger human life always stands in, the common prayer is 'Lead us not into temptation'; 'Do not bring us to the test'; or Banquo's, 'Merciful powers | Restrain in me . . .' With any luck the prayers will be answered, the 'merciful powers' *will* mobilize, *will* get stuck in, *will* come to our aid. But what if they don't? Are we all potential Macbeths? When Macduff was trying to comprehend the slaughter of his family, he suddenly asked, 'Did heaven look on | And would not take their part?' (IV.3.222–3). That is a partner question to Macbeth's, all that time ago: 'Why?' Why was he stopped 'Upon this blasted heath . . . With such prophetic greeting?' Why was *he* targeted? Did heaven look on and would not take his part? Where were the merciful powers when Macbeth needed them?

The bleakness we take away from *Macbeth* resides not just in our knowledge that Macbeth destroyed himself: he chose darkness, and 'when once our grace we have forgot, | Nothing goes right. We would, and we would not' (*Measure for Measure*, IV.4.31–2). But we have seen, too, the aloofness of the heavens while the 'instruments of darkness' were busy meddling with Macbeth to the ruin of his life. We know he did not do what he did unprompted. In one version of the play's final stage picture, this tragedy reproduces the deep ambivalence of our response – and gives us a sight to fear. The body of the 'dead butcher' (V.6.108), and all the dark past that body represents, lies onstage. But alongside it is the body of his last victim, Seyward's boy. It represents the future: the body of a child.

A NOTE ON THE ENDING(S)

Every production, indeed every reading, will decide how to stage the ending of *Macbeth*, but if we turn to the Folio for direction, we discover that vestiges of two different endings are embedded in the 'original' text of this play. Either that, or the spoken text is intact, but there are at least two significant gaps in the stage directions that produce discrepancies in the onstage action.

After Folio line 2475 (V.6.73 in the present edition) the stage direction indicates that Macbeth and Macduff '*Exeunt fighting. Alarums*'. The next line is another stage direction that, rather bafflingly, has the just-exited combatants return: '*Enter Fighting, and Macbeth slaine*'. Immediately after comes a further stage direction: '*Retreat, and Flourish. Enter with Drumme and Colours, Malcolm, Seyward, Rosse, Thanes, & Soldiers*'. From these instructions, it looks as if Macbeth is killed onstage, Malcolm and the rest entering to find Macduff standing over the corpse. But, if so, Malcolm's entrance line is puzzling: 'I would the friends we miss were safe arrived'

(V.6.74). Some twenty lines later, the Macduff he says is 'missing' (77) turns up. Another stage direction after Folio line 2503 (V.6.92) indicates: '*Enter Macduffe with Macbeth's head*'. But this surely suggests that Macbeth is killed offstage, that once the combatants '*Exeunt fighting*' at line 73, they don't return. In sum, either Macbeth dies onstage, his body lying in full view, registering significant meaning for spectators until the end (an ending that will require some judicious cutting of Malcolm's text around line 74), or he dies offstage, where the 'butcher' is butchered (108), and his mutilated head returns after line 92, perhaps one final uncanny visual joke, if spectators recognize it as the '*Armed Head*' that rose from the Weird Sisters' cauldron in Act IV, scene 1.

Of course, it is possible to smooth over (or muddy) these textual discrepancies and the actorly choices they prompt. Notice, for example, that the present edition wants *both* endings, '*Macbeth slain*' (73) and '*Macbeth's head*' brought on (92). To achieve this, the editor fills the gap he sees in the Folio's directions by interpolating a new stage direction, '*Exit Macduff*' after '*Macbeth slain*' – but does not go on to indicate what function, logically, Macduff's (new) exit is designed to serve, that is, to remove Macbeth's corpse. (For more on these matters, see the Commentary on V.6.73, p. 153).

One final scenic contradiction remains. Where is Young Seyward? The boy soldier who enters at V.6.15 bristling with courage to fight his maiden battle is killed only seven lines later. Does his dead body remain onstage? There is no stage direction for its removal in the Folio (or in the present edition) and, indeed, no one to carry it off except Macbeth, who rather taunts the corpse – 'Thou wast born of woman' (21) – before exiting than offering it honourable recovery. Later, however, when

Ross, entering with Malcolm, Old Seyward and the victorious army, has to announce the boy's death, he says the corpse has been 'brought off the field' (83). So perhaps another stage direction is missing. Perhaps Young Seyward's body has been cleared. Or perhaps not. Maybe it lies onstage, the dead child kept apart from his father by some poignant blocking and strategic cutting of the spoken text, a mute counter-image to the other body that, in some stagings, will lie there too, the body of the king-killing child-killer.

Carol Chillington Rutter

The Play in Performance

Macbeth is Shakespeare's most compact, most relentless tragedy. Half the length of *Hamlet* – 2,100 lines vs. 3,900 lines – *Macbeth* can be played straight through with few cuts and no interval in under two hours – as both the Royal Shakespeare Company (1986, directed by Adrian Noble) and Northern Broadsides (2002, directed by Barrie Rutter) have shown. It is a play delivered in short, sharp shocks, and its restlessness, near breathlessness, are effects of the playwright's design. This is a play Shakespeare has composed of brief encounters. Only seven of the play's twenty-six scenes have more than a hundred lines, and six have fewer than thirty. To think about what Shakespeare is doing structurally in *Macbeth*, compare *A Midsummer Night's Dream*, a play about the same length (2,200 lines) but delivered in nine scenes. Or for contrast see *Othello*, written a couple years before *Macbeth*. Its massive 3,600 lines compose only fifteen scenes. Also, put *Macbeth*'s punchiness – the 10-line opening scene, the 23-line Banquo assassination scene – against, for example, the epic sweep of *Titus Andronicus'* opening scene – 635 lines – or the leisurely sprawl – 443 lines – of a scene like Act II, scene 4 in *Henry IV, Part I*. Shakespeare knows how to write 'big' scenes. Writing scenes like *Macbeth*'s, as if they were gulps for air, is a conscious choice. So notice that *Macbeth*'s 'biggest' scene, almost an antidote to the rest of the play, is Act IV, scene 3, set in England, where the 'king-becoming graces' (91) are anatomized and where a nameless physician passes briefly over the stage, his seemingly gratuitous function to report what is happening elsewhere: the English King Edward's 'miraculous work' curing 'a crew of wretched souls' of a disease called 'the Evil' (141, 146). But like other seeming irrelevancies in this stripped-down narrative (Ross discussing the weather with an anonymous Old Man in Act II, scene 4, Lennox sarcastically trading gossip in Act III, scene 6, the Porter inventing the early modern version of the 'knock, knock' joke in Act II, scene 3) this diversion turns out to be utterly to the point.

While Shakespeare-the-wordwright seems to have been taking it easy in *Macbeth*, scripting a tragedy so 'cabined, cribbed, confined' (III.4.23) that some editors have thought the play that has come down to us must be a shortened touring version, his partner, Shakespeare-the-designer, was working overtime. The sense-battering sights and sounds he scripts for *Macbeth* challenge the technical limits of production – on our stage as much as Shakespeare's Globe. He wants '*Thunder and lightning*', '*Witches*' to '*vanish*', a ghost, a coronation banquet set then '*dispersed*', apparitions and hallucinations, a decapitated head offered up at the end along with the crown. He requires quantities of blood. And at least three stunning costume changes: at III.1.10, when Macbeth enters '*as King*', perhaps in Duncan's 'borrowed robes'; at V.1.18, when his guilty Lady enters from bed in the dress of 'innocent sleep', holding a candle up to her crimes; and at V.3.33–54, a blackly comic sequence that has the deranged tyrant first bellow for his armour and order himself dressed – restoring momentarily a skewed image of the 'noble' soldier Macbeth – then immediately shriek for it to be pulled off, marking a mind giddied and a reputation that no longer fits. Some of *Macbeth*'s terrifying sensations are effects of the text and its imagery; others are performed. Images of blood and sleep, for example, travel through the play-text but also have enacted presence onstage: spectators see these images played out in front of them. Not least among such visual effects are those produced by doubling: sixteen players can perform *Macbeth*'s thirty-odd roles. Does Duncan return as the Old Man and the two Doctors? Is Lady Macduff one of the Witches? Does the 'devil-porter' double Seyton (pronounced 'Satan'?), Macbeth's sole comrade at the end – or does Duncan double them both? And are such doubles blank to spectators, merely practical, or do we read the layering of roles as significant? What might it mean if, while Duncan's corpse is lying murdered next door, the actor who played Duncan enters to answer the knocking at the gate in Act II, scene 3?

'STANDS SCOTLAND WHERE IT DID?'

Shakespeare's Scotland is a place on the map, a place where civilization cedes to desolation across a scoured, eye-baffling terrain. But it is also a space in the mind, accessed via confession and soliloquy. Film is the medium that can locate Shakespeare's 'real' Scotland most satisfactorily – Roman Polanski's 1971 *Macbeth* possibly the best in this pictorially realist genre, his camera tracking human figures struggling across a wild landscape of dissolving mists, ebbing tides and sudden rock formations that naturally produce weird optical illusions. But cinema can also take spectators in the opposite direction, into stylization, as if exploring the mental interiors discovered in Macbeth's self-reckonings: in Akira Kurosawa's eerily silent 1957 expressionist film, *Kumonosu-ju* (*Throne of Blood*), Scotland is 'The Castle of the Spider's Web' – the literal translation of the film's Japanese title – set inside a tangled, vegetation-trailing forest where, no matter how hard he spurs his horse in another direction, Washizu always arrives back at the clearing where an ancient, sexless crone sits turning by hand a bamboo spinning wheel, like Clotho, the Fate in Greek mythology who spins the thread of man's life. In the theatre *Macbeth*'s best directors find ways of translating into physical space the play's claustrophobia, supernatural strangeness and headlong rush: in 1976 Trevor Nunn set *Macbeth* (RSC at The Other Place) on black floorboards inside a white circle – a tight 'wooden O' which took on multiple meanings. It was an occult cipher, a rehearsal space, a child's playground marked with 'in' and 'out', a space enclosing inner terror. This studio-sized production set its simple theatrical effects in plain view of the audience. (Duncan's royal robes hung from a tailor's dummy; a thunder sheet, from above.) It made characters 'off' observers of the tragedy. (Macduff stood outside the circle watching the slaughter of his family.) And its 'sights' were ones that mimicked the doubleness of Macbeth's encounters with strangeness: the Witches 'vanished' when they stepped outside the circle – yet were still *there*, and visible to spectators. In 1986, on Stratford's main stage, Adrian Noble set the play in a black box whose walls moved in on the killer, shrinking his world to a cell before it was smashed apart by Macduff in a *Seven Samurai*-style final assault (an homage to Kurosawa) that splintered walls and floorboards. In 1999 Gregory Doran, like Nunn, conceived *Macbeth* as a chamber play. For him a big theatre breathes too much air around the action of *Macbeth*, so he opted to direct it in the RSC's Swan, on a near-empty stage, but made the theatre a labyrinth, its aisles, gangways, stairs and galleries an assault course or rat run. These became the physical correlative to mental torture and moral vertigo. And the witches were always around, behind or underneath the action, ready to break through the surface of the stage and overturn the tyrant's shaky hold on order by toppling the piece of furniture that symbolized it, his dining table. For directors who read *Macbeth* as a contemporary history play – its politics topical, its dress modern, its people versions of 'us' – 'Scotland' stands for 'tyrannies' closer to home: for Michael Bogdanov (in his 1998 TV film starring Sean Pertwee), what Margaret Thatcher had made of Britain, a smouldering rubbish heap piled high with the affluent trash of a 'gimme-gimme-gimme' society. For Penny Woolcock, in her made-for-television *Macbeth on the Estate* (1997), shot on an inner-city Birmingham housing estate, 'Scotland' was a violent, drug-wrecked wasteland, and the 'estate' was a metaphor for the current 'estate' of the nation. As these citations show, the afterlife of Shakespeare's *Macbeth* turns Macduff's question – 'Stands Scotland where it did?' (IV.3.164) – into a constantly renewing challenge for performance.

'HELL IS MURKY!'

Shakespeare sets *Macbeth* almost entirely in the dark – darkness being an effect he evokes on the full-daylight Globe stage with torches (called for in stage directions throughout the Folio text). Doran's production achieved this same effect with terrifying immediacy, opening by plunging the theatre into total blackout. This sensory deprivation for the audience was acute and instructive, an anticipation of the moral, emotional blackout Macbeth was going to encounter. (By contrast, one of the things that makes Woolcock's take on *Macbeth* so bleak is that the drug pushing, the gang warfare, the queasy homosociability and sheer brutishness of testosterone-fuelled intimidation and violence on the estate: all this is traffic conducted in broad daylight.) Shakespeare's strategy in *Macbeth* seems to be to starve the spectator's retina of stimulation then to flood it with intense exposures to colour: a lightning flash at the beginning; the '*bleeding Captain*' in scene 2. That Captain stands before us for fifty lines, a 'thing of blood' (like Caius Martius after Corioli in *Coriolanus*), registering the 'acceptable' face of killing. Later, red will return to shock the eye when it is misapplied, when first Macbeth then his wife enters bloody-handed. And again in Act IV, scene 1 when a '*Bloody Child*' rises from the Witches' cauldron – covered in birth blood or death blood? At the end, the blood image perhaps transfers to Macduff. The fist that holds up Macbeth's severed head or wrenches the crown from his corpse: is it now as bloody as the hand that killed Duncan?

For sheer contrast, directors, following Shakespeare's cues, find light in the darkness. Nunn made Duncan – white haired, white bearded, dressed in sacrificial white – the antithesis to Macbeth's blackness, more a penitent than a king, even his heavy embroidered coronation robes more ecclesiastical than temporal. Noble set Act IV, scene 2 under white lights, in the Macduff nursery, where the children, in pure white nightgowns, golden-haired and radiant as angels, played before bedtime, one of them fooling with the assassin's black boot straps before being picked up and stabbed. Doran set the same scene in the household's laundry, the children at bath time, amidst clothes horses drying white towels and washing lines draped with white sheets; Bogdanov put the ambush in a white room, the children hunched over bowls of porridge; Woolcock set it in the Macduff kitchen. (Marking a growing sense of pain and incomprehension at atrocity, contemporary productions of *Macbeth* increasingly locate our culture's revulsion against casual violence, terrorism and the slaughter of innocents in the killing of Macduff's children. In Woolcock's film, Macbeth himself killed the children. A close-up on the wailing face of Macduff's baby girl, strapped into her pushchair, saw her big eyes wide with tears and terror as, out of shot, her mother and brother were battered to death; then a cut to Macbeth watched him whisper 'thou egg' and raise his knife. In Calixto Bieito's urban gangland Theatre Romea production (Barcelona, 2002), one of the children was drowned in the paddling pool kept by the (childless) Macbeths in their back garden for when Macduff's kids came round to play. The second was battered to death with a Coca-Cola bottle. The third would have survived, hidden behind the sofa, if the assassins, on their way out, had not heard his recorder. They gripped him tight and smothered him with his teddy bear.) Later, this limited palette – black, white, red – will extend to green: the leafy camouflage of Birnam Wood that screens Malcolm's advance but that perhaps, too, gestures symbolically at growth. Green seems to be sprouting from the blasted heath (however ambivalently, for, after all, the branches are cut). Other colours flare briefly out of the gloom: the golden crown, the little yellow halo around the sleepwalker's candle. Some directors find extraordinary beauty in *Macbeth*. In Yukio Ninagawa's Japanese adaptation (1985) cherry blossom fell as men were murdered, drifting like snow across the stage.

'DIDST THOU NOT HEAR A NOISE?'

The *Times* theatre critic Irving Wardle has called *Macbeth* 'the best radio play Shakespeare ever wrote', not simply because it demands so much from the imagination but because it is backed by a 'hair-raising sound-score'. Thunder announces each entrance of the Weird Sisters; alarums and drums cue the armies' progress in Acts I and V, six '*Alarums*' marked in Act V, scene 6 alone. '*Hautboys*' – oboes, used on Shakespeare's stage for solemn, stately music – play as the banquet is laid (I.7) – and again as the '*show of eight kings*' passes over the stage (IV.1.110). A bell strikes (II.1.61) – it is both a summons and a knell – then (II.3.77) it clangs a blood-curdling alarm. Not just sights but noises appal *Macbeth*: an owl shrieks, crickets cry, a man shouts 'Murder' in his sleep, a mother grabs her babies and runs screaming from their slaughtermen. Sighs, groans, 'Lamentings . . . i'the air' (II.3.53) supply a metaphysical acoustic to Duncan's murder. But there is plenty of noise on the ground, too: the sounds Macbeth's thugs make as they pulp Banquo – it takes so long to kill a man!; the animal wail that rises out of Lady Macbeth, sleepwalking: 'Oh! Oh! Oh!' (V.1.49); the '*cry within of women*' that reminds sense-deadened Macbeth of 'the taste of fears' (V.5.7, 9). And in that awful moment of silence after the murder – II.2.57 – when he is left alone with only his bloody hands for company, gazing at their witness of his crime, there is the heart-stopping noise – banging loud enough to wake the dead? – that sends stomachs into mouths (ours as well as his) and terror down spines. Shakespeare's scripting of the knocking at the gate is brilliant: there are ten sound cues – '*Knock*' or '*Knock within*' – in the Folio text between II.2.57 and II.3.18 that simultaneously ratchet up tension and drain it away, as we hear the knocking first with Macbeth's ears, then the Porter's, whose tedious brief comedy of delay makes us scream. But not with fear. With frustration. The forces of discovery are right there on the other side of the door! They could catch the killer red-handed – but can't get in! (That, of course, is the point. The pause between murder and discovery that stretches our nerves to breaking point, first sending the scene into overdrive then stalling it when the drunken Porter slouches in, is both thematic and practical. It plays upon ideas of guilt,disclosure and timing, while giving the Globe's tire-man – or today's theatre dresser – time to get Macbeth into his nightgown and the blood off his hands before he is needed to re-enter at II.3.39.)

Do we hear the Witches producing a weird kind of music in *Macbeth* – a sister sound to Ophelia's tuneless ballad in *Hamlet* or Desdemona's plaintive willow song in *Othello*? Northern Broadsides put the Weird Sisters in wooden clogs, so their wayward speech rhythms were acoustically echoed in their footfalls every time they moved. Cheek by Jowl (1987) made them pure sound – fingers drumming on theatre floorboards, a bow scraped across violin strings. Nunn set their sing-song incantation (I.3.31) against Duncan at prayer, their rising crescendo and blood-quickening tempo like a satanic antiphon, drowning out the confession the Priest-King intoned, 'Mea culpa, mea culpa.'

Undoubtedly the strangest sound that comes out of *Macbeth* is laughter. Macbeth hears it from next door while he is killing Duncan. Someone – a groom? Malcolm? – 'did laugh in's sleep' (II.2.22). And he may hear it right at the end. Does Macduff answer Macbeth's warning, 'I bear a charmèd life', by laughing in his face across a half-line pause before answering, 'Despair thy charm' (V.6.51–2)? Antony Sher's Macbeth in Doran's production saw the joke far earlier (III.4.140) when his wife, salvaging what she could of the ghastly dinner party, tried fixing a home remedy, like a plaster, on his hurt mind: 'You lack the season of all natures, sleep.' This man, who had murdered sleep, turned on her, amazed: a cure, in *sleep*? He started laughing, 'Come, we'll to *sleep*': the idea was hilarious. Then so did she. Locked in each other's arms, they rocked like demented children, their laughter drying into convulsive gulps.

'NO MORE SIGHTS!'

By Act IV, scene 1 Macbeth wants not just to know the future but to see it. But as soon as he has, he wants 'no more sights!' (154). So what does he see? On the Globe stage the '*Armed Head*', the '*Bloody Childe*' and the '*Childe Crowned, with a Tree in his hand*' described in the Folio stage directions were probably acted, those playing the apparitions coming up through a trap in the stage floor to rise out of the cauldron. Each of them later '*descends*', and the cauldron 'sinks' (105), giving way to another 'show', '*of eight Kings, and Banquo last, with a glasse in his hand*'. These apparitions are real, not, like the 'air-drawn dagger', 'Impostors to true fear' (III.4.61, 63). And yet: if the dagger was a 'false creation', isn't it possible that the apparitions are hallucinations, too, 'Proceeding' from Macbeth's 'heat-oppressèd brain'? (II.1.38–9). After all, Lady Macbeth did not see Banquo's ghost in Act III, scene 4 – as spectators did not see the dagger in Act II, scene 1.

Shakespeare quite deliberately makes these things ambiguous, for he is playing with ideas about foresight, insight, eyesight and sightlessness, and subsequent performances will have to decide where to draw the line between the imagined and the material. In Ninagawa, dead Duncan was remembered ceremonially in his full suit of Samurai armour that sat on a dais, looking on to the banquet. The ghost appeared when a revolve suddenly turned and the armour was horribly occupied – by dead Banquo. In Noble, Jonathan Pryce's Macbeth alone saw the ghost. When he did, he sent the banquet sprawling by grabbing up the white tablecloth, splaying it out in front of him like a shield, a gesture that 'produced' the ghost to spectators' eyes. At the RSC in 2004 (directed by Dominic Cooke) Banquo's ghost was almost comically real, a bloody busybody stalking the feast, but the apparitions and show of kings were giant holograms, projected over Macbeth's head. In Doran's *Macbeth* the stage walls grew rubbery, the apparitions, like sci-fi parasites trapped in host bodies, leered out, literally stretching the boundaries of the real. In 1976, thrown flat on his back and forced to choke down a chalice full of the witches' noxious brew, Ian McKellen's Macbeth (directed by Nunn) produced each of the apparitions out of himself. Weirdly human, doll-sized fetishes held over his drugged head seemed to drag up from somewhere deep inside him choked, strangled voices that uttered each prediction. In Noble's 1986 production the Witches' operatives were children. They entered, giggling, in white nightgowns, to a Macbeth who was blindfolded with a napkin soaked in the hell-broth that, absorbed through the eyes, went straight to the brain, producing hallucinations that possessed the bodies of children. They dodged Macbeth's groping hands to deliver their predictions to his muffled ears, the littlest climbing up on the big man's knee to whisper what Macbeth – role-reversed into a ventriloquist's dummy – spoke out loud. In the following scene these angel babies – or toxic 'familiars' – doubled Macduff's children.

It is not just the sensational 'sights' that performance needs to pay attention to in *Macbeth* but the scenic doubles which complicate our spectatorship with mirror scenes that work by repetition to reiterate, contrast, intensify or generalize ideas, and to focus energies or to disperse them. There are two (maybe three) banquets; two physicians; two crowned kings; two armed heads; two wives and mothers; a whole run of sons; two armies; two kingdoms; at the end, two dead bodies, Macbeth's and young Seyward's. Does the theatre see these as *like* each other – or different?

'WHO'S THERE?'

Shakespeare's roles are wonderfully elastic and open to a wide range of actorly interpretation, their limits tolerant of any number of performances. That said, Antony Sher, who played Macbeth in 1999, calls the part 'the dark actor's Hamlet': unlike the Dane, he wryly observes, the Thane is rarely cast blond. But citing Hamlet, Sher is pointing to something more important in the role: that Macbeth is a thinker, a loner turning over possibility in a string of soliloquies that show the 'man of action' grappling 'constantly with the head, the great visionary brain, that gorgeous damaged imagination'. If an imagination like Leontes' in *The Winter's Tale* is, says Sher, 'something painted by Bosch' that 'teems with horrid little sticky pink nudes', Macbeth's imagination 'is by Dali: elegant, epic pictures of lonely figures in empty landscapes – a newborn baby carried on the wind, one bloody hand turning the sea red, a queue of pointless tomorrows shuffling towards oblivion'.

Sher's Macbeth went from triumphalist commando – a Vietnam or Gulf War general in black beret and battle fatigues, carried shoulder-high alongside Banquo by their whooping squaddies, themselves high on violence, and all of them with faces streaked in blood, sweat and filth – to groomed courtier at formal dinner, gleaming in black tie and tails (literally undone when he rolled up his shirt sleeve to kill Duncan), to something out of Beckett. In his bunker in Act V, his crown awry, the 'throne' he sat on was an old suitcase. Jonathan Pryce played a Macbeth who lurched from war hero to psychopath to clown. He first entered armour-plated and draped in black-and-white tartan, then became oddly clerical in a black cassock, finally, absurd, in huge boots and slack stockings: the joke the Weird Sisters had played on his mind was written on this Macbeth's buffoonish body by the end. Ian McKellen was a sleek, reptilian Macbeth in black leather who leaped on a chair to grab the naked light bulb that was suspended from a flex over the playing space. On 'Tomorrow, and tomorrow, and tomorrow', he sent it drunkenly swinging, turning himself into a lurching shadow, a monstrous player casting dark images over all the walls of the theatre. By contrast James Frain's Macbeth in Woolcock was an urban thug in blue jeans, wielding a baseball bat. Macbeth can be 'fascinating' and 'flawed' but heroic (Laurence Olivier in Glen Byam Shaw's 1955 production), sex-driven (Nicol Williamson directed by Nunn in 1974), a natural-born killer (Jon

Finch directed by Polanski), the epitome of the feudal
warrior caste (Hira's samurai Macbeth in Ninagawa).

But he cannot work alone. He needs a 'partner of greatness' (I.5.9–10). Almost no one any longer sees Lady
Macbeth as the female fiend and evil genius invented by
Sarah Siddons (opposite John Philip Kemble's 'nerveless'
Macbeth in 1785), who nagged her husband to murder –
and terrified spectators, one of whom commented of her
sleepwalking scene, 'Well sir, I smelt blood. I swear I
smelt blood.' Helen Faucit (in the 1860s) made Lady
Macbeth domestic, gentle; Ellen Terry (in the 1880s),
bright, audacious, 'pungent', said a contemporary review,
'with the *odeur de femme*' – and strong, if the John Singer
Sargent portrait of Terry as Lady Macbeth is anything
to go by. Later Ladies have been more vulnerable: Vivien
Leigh, frail, almost too slight to drag her coronation robe
(Byam Shaw); Judi Dench, entering at a run, repeating
excitedly the words of the letter she had read so many
times she knew it by heart, terrified by the spirits she
summoned, her cries in her sleepwalking – 'Oh! Oh! Oh!'
– the sound of a soul being flayed from its body (Nunn,
1976); Sinead Cusack, a girl in a green dress who slept
in her husband's old pullover when he went into the field
and who, in the sleepwalking scene, set her candle 'down'
in mid-air as her distraction fixed on her hands – her
gentlewoman lunging to catch it as it fell (Noble); Harriet
Walter, brittle, wounded, smoothing her husband's dress
uniform, carefully lifted from a suitcase, talking to it –
'Glamis thou art' (Doran). For recent actors (Cusack,
Walter, Susan Vidler in Woolcock), the secret sorrow
driving Lady Macbeth is located in that line 'I have given
suck' that puts in her personal history the death of a baby.

All the play's parts are similarly 'open' to performance choices. Duncan: a priest-king (Griffith Jones in

Nunn, 1976); a mafia boss (Rod Steiger in the 1955 film, *Joe Macbeth*); an honoured patriarch (Joseph O'Conor in Doran); a bloated, superannuated skinhead presiding over urban blight (Ray Winstone in Woolcock). His son: a swaggering punk or Sandhurst's best or a gormless 'nice guy' genuinely stunned to be named Prince of Cumberland. Banquo: solid or slippery, invulnerable to suggestion or as much tempted as Macbeth. (John Woodvine in Nunn's production stood gazing into his young son's face as he whispered 'Merciful powers, | Restrain in me the cursèd thoughts . . .' (II.1.7–8): he was brooding on the Witches' predictions – seeing this child as Scotland's future king – and beginning to wonder how he might hurry the prediction along.) Macduff: bluff, bewildered, or protected by a mind that simply doesn't think as far as Macbeth's. And then there are the Witches. They were battlefield scavengers in Theodore Komisarjevsky's modern-dress production in 1933, when the Somme was still recent history. Noble remembered this image in 1986: his Witches scoured the battlefield looting corpses – and salvaged from the carnage a child survivor whom they hustled away as booty. In 1976 Nunn saw them as the 'triple Hecat'. They represented a dark female force, more potent than masculinity, that was located in the combined power of the 'virgin', the 'mother' and the 'crone'. The young witch was an idiot whose twisted face and spittle-ringed mouth was yet hauntingly beautiful. The maternal witch rocked her when her trances tortured her while the old one looked on, impassive. In Doran's production, the Witches were urban scum, filthy, feral, matted, quick, always on the move, dodging across lights like rats over-running the spoil heap left behind by modern guerilla war. Perhaps most fearfully for today's audiences, the Witches in

Penny Woolcock's *Macbeth on the Estate* were children.

A Jacobean tragedy, a royal history play, a social documentary for modern times: *Macbeth* is a play that leaves spectators with questions about the future. Can what has been done be undone? Will the future be different – or more of the same? In Polanski's film the final shots watched Donalbain, now next-in-blood to his brother-king, ride off to find the Witches. In Orson Welles's film of 1948, as the crown rolled from Macbeth's fallen head, little Fleance reached out to clutch it. In 1999, directed by Doran, the boy Fleance was left at the end holding a fetish, a memento from the Witches; in 2004, in Cooke's production, he was the last to exit. He heard a whine in the air, hesitated, turned back – saw the Witches and froze. In Woolcock's 1997 film, standing in long shot on the rubble-strewn wasteground against the skyline of the estate that was also the nation, Macduff spoke the ending: 'Alas, poor country. Almost afraid to know itself.' Then he turned and walked away.

Carol Chillington Rutter

Further Reading

Among single-volume editions, A. R. Braunmuller's New Cambridge edition (1997) is currently the most useful but does not altogether replace Kenneth Muir's Arden edition (1951; last revised 1984). There is an interestingly argued Oxford edition (1990), with elaborate apparatus, edited by Nicholas Brooke; among paperbacks, one should mention the revised Bantam, edited by David Bevington (1988); G. L. Kittredge's edition (1936) is worth consulting for the well-focused fullness of its annotations. The Harrow edition of Watkins and Lemmon (1964) concentrates on the theatrical possibilities of the play, illustrated by line drawings of Globe-type performances. A comprehensive account of scholarship and criticism is to be found in *'Macbeth': An Annotated Bibliography* by Thomas Wheeler (The Garland Shakespeare Bibliographies, 1990).

SOURCES

The relevant passages from Holinshed's *Chronicle*, the principal source, are printed in Furness's New Variorum edition (1873), in Kenneth Muir's and in Nicholas Brooke's. Geoffrey Bullough's *Narrative and Dramatic*

Sources of Shakespeare, vol. VII (1973), discusses and prints all known sources and analogues.

THE PLAY

(1) *Classic Criticism*

Brian Vickers's *Shakespeare: The Cultural Heritage*, in six volumes (1974–81), presents substantial extracts from theatrical and literary comments up to 1801. The most famous literary essay on *Macbeth* – De Quincey's 'On the Knocking on the Gate in *Macbeth*' – is available (slightly abbreviated) in Furness. R. G. Moulton's *Shakespeare as a Dramatic Artist* (1885) remains the most pertinently accessible of Victorian treatments. Moulton's 'arrangement' of *Macbeth* as a Greek tragedy (in *The Ancient Classical Drama* (1890)) is a stimulating exercise in comparative criticism. Scholarship that opens up the background of the play can be sampled in Walter Clyde Curry's essay on 'Demonic Metaphysics' in his *Shakespeare's Philosophical Patterns* (1937), in Willard Farnham's *Shakespeare's Tragic Frontier* (1950) and in H. N. Paul, *The Royal Play of 'Macbeth'* (1950) – but see the comments on Paul in Muir's Appendix D and in the Appendix to Chapter 8 in J. R. Brown's *Focus on 'Macbeth'* (1981). A. C. Bradley's chapter in *Shakespearean Tragedy* (1904) remains unsurpassed in its accurate attention to detail coupled with a coherent and lucid theoretical basis. But, in so far as this coherence depends on a subordination of the poetry spoken to the person speaking, it has excited rejection, first in L. C. Knights's 1933 essay 'How Many Children Had Lady Macbeth?' – reprinted in *Explorations* (1946) – and subsequently in many works

concerned to validate the images in the play as the source
of its inner meaning, as in Cleanth Brooks's 'The Naked
Babe and the Cloak of Manliness' in *The Well-Wrought
Urn* (1942) and in G. Wilson Knight's *The Wheel of Fire*
(1930) and *The Imperial Theme* (1931). E. M. W. Tillyard
pointed out *Macbeth*'s relation to the history plays in his
Shakespeare's History Plays (1944).

(2) *Modernist Criticism*

Judged by the size of the bibliography, *Macbeth* seems in
the last four decades to have attracted less critical interest
than the other 'Bradleyan' tragedies – *Othello*, *King Lear*
and *Hamlet*. The classical simplicity of the plot, what
Emrys Jones (*Scenic Form in Shakespeare* (1971)) has called
the 'elegance' and 'formal coherence' of its plotting and
the apparent determinism of its moral structure, with
good and evil placed at opposite poles, may have discour-
aged further essays in description. Modernist criticism
has chosen to go behind the apparently tidy coherence
that classic criticism described, concentrating, like the
New Critics of the 1930s, on the disruptive energy that
emerges in the poetry of the play. But the modernists are
less interested in describing this as part of a moral pattern
than as an indicator of the suppressed energies of political groups opposed to the Stuart kings. Feminism and
radical politics (not always separable) have provided the
principal vocabularies for this enterprise.

The feminist mode finds an obvious justification in the
play's recurrent interest in 'manliness' (violent soldiership) and in its exploration of the consequences of this
in the contrasting fates of husband and wife. Freud had
given his blessing to this enquiry in a brief discussion on
the effect of 'success' in fragmenting character (a point

taken up again in Barbara Everett's *Young Hamlet* (1989)).
Freud is particularly concerned with the incoherence of
the victim-wife, Lady Macbeth (see *The Standard Edition
of the Complete Works*, vol. 4 (1957), pp. 318–24). Janet
Adelman – in *Cannibals, Witches and Divorce* (1987), ed.
Marjorie Garber – replaces Bradley's moral universals
with Freud's psychological ones and sees Macbeth's career
as a history of psychic disorientation, requiring him to
take refuge in the fantasy of total maleness in order to
cope with female domination (appearing in both the
Witches and Lady Macbeth). For actors' accounts of
playing Lady Macbeth in the decade that first exposed
Shakespeare on stage to feminist scrutiny, see Carol
Chillington Rutter, *Clamorous Voices: Shakespeare's
Women Today* (1988).

The disruption of 'conformist' views produced by
reading the play from the point of view of gender politics can also be achieved in more purely historical terms.
The recentness of the Gunpowder Plot of 1605 and the
trials of Jesuit 'traitors' (referred to in the Porter's speech)
have suggested to some that the play has a hidden political agenda. See Stephen Mullaney's article in *English
Literary History* 47 (1980), pp. 32–47. David Norbrook's
essay on *Macbeth*, printed in K. Sharpe and S. Zwicker,
Politics of Discourse (1987), argues against the classic
position that the play turns on an absolute contrast
between the tyrant Macbeth and the good king Duncan.
He finds in the background of the play and in Scottish
history (drawing on Arthur M. Clark's *Murder under
Trust* (1981)) evidence of anti-monarchical currents of
thought and deduces Shakespeare's imaginative sympathy
with such thoughts. Alan Sinfield in *Faultlines* (1992)
offers a very similar view (Duncan is delegitimized by
the violence needed to sustain him; in a world sustained

by violence Macbeth has no other way of expressing political opposition). Compare also the essay by Michael Hawkins in John R. Brown's *Focus on Macbeth* (1981).

Brown's collection concentrates mainly on what may be called 'the psychology of performance' (see especially Robin Grove's 'Multiplying Villainies of Nature'). Sinfield's more recent collection of essays focuses on modernist positions. For essays that combine the two approaches and that understand the subversive energies of Shakespearian drama to be released in onstage performances rather than in social contexts, see John Kerrigan's *On Shakespeare and Early Modern Literature* (2001). *Shakespeare Survey 19* (1966) is devoted to *Macbeth* and contains a survey of critical studies; many of the essays in the volume are reprinted in *Aspects of 'Macbeth'* (1977), ed. Kenneth Muir and Philip Edwards. *Shakespeare Survey 57* (2004) is devoted to '*Macbeth* and Its Afterlife'; see particularly Carol Chillington Rutter's 'Remind Me: How Many Children Had Lady Macbeth?' R. A. Foakes has an excellent bibliographical essay in Stanley Wells's *Shakespeare: A Bibliographical Guide* (1990).

STAGE HISTORY

Stage history has occupied more space than usual in recent writings on *Macbeth*, perhaps because theatre allows more scope for a free play of interpretation. Stage history is discussed in Braunmuller's New Cambridge edition, in Brooke's Oxford edition and in A. C. Sprague's *Shakespeare and the Actors* (1944). For a brilliant hands-on introduction to the play's performance requirements that, even where it is dated, remains illuminating, see Harley Granville Barker's *Prefaces to Shakespeare*, vol.

VI (1923). Dennis Bartholomeusz's *Macbeth and the Players* (1969) gives an illuminating account of stage actions from 1610 to 1964. Marvin Rosenberg, in *The Masks of 'Macbeth'* (1978), takes the reader through the play and at each point describes various theatrical realizations. Gordon Williams, in *'Macbeth': Text and Performance* (1985), offers a useful set of summary points. For a highly readable comparative study of the play in performance, see Bernice W. Kliman's *Shakespeare in Performance: 'Macbeth'* (1992), and for more on contemporary performance, see relevant essays in *Shakespeare Survey 57*. The most informative actor's account of playing Macbeth is Antony Sher's in *Beside Myself* (2001). The Cornmarket Press has issued facsimiles of playhouse texts for 1671, 1673, 1674, 1753, 1761 and 1794. The manuscript of Middleton's *The Witch* is printed as a Malone Society Reprint (1948–50), eds. W. W. Greg and F. P. Wilson. The Witch scenes from *The Witch* are printed in Furness. Davenant's operatic version (written before 1668, published in 1674) appears in Furness, in Christopher Spencer's *Five Restoration Adaptations of Shakespeare* (1965) and in a full scholarly edition by the same author in 1961.

The Orson Welles, Polanski and Kurosawa films are available on video cassette and DVD, as are films made from Trevor Nunn's (1976) and Gregory Doran's (1999) Royal Shakespeare Company productions of *Macbeth*. Of interest, too, are *Macbeth* spin-off films available commercially, *Men of Respect* (1991) and *Scotland, PA* (2001). Many of these films are discussed in Russell Jackson's *The Cambridge Companion to Shakespeare on Film* (2000), which also points students to further reading in the growing area of Shakespeare film studies.

THE TRAGEDY OF MACBETH

The Characters in the Play

Duncan, KING of Scotland

MALCOLM
DONALBAIN } his sons

MACBETH, Thane of Glamis, later of Cawdor, later King
  of Scotland

BANQUO
MACDUFF
LENNOX
ROSS } Thanes of Scotland
MENTETH
ANGUS
CATHNESS

FLEANCE, Banquo's son
SEYWARD, Earl of Northumberland
YOUNG SEYWARD, his son
SEYTON, Macbeth's armour-bearer
SON of Macduff
A CAPTAIN
An English DOCTOR
A Scottish DOCTOR
A PORTER
An OLD MAN

LADY Macbeth
WIFE of Macduff
GENTLEWOMAN attendant on Lady Macbeth
FIRST WITCH
SECOND WITCH ⎫ three Weird Sisters
THIRD WITCH ⎭
Three other witches
HECAT
APPARITIONS

Three MURDERERS
Other MURDERERS

MESSENGERS
SERVANTS
LORDS
SOLDIERS
Gentlemen, officers, attendants

Thunder and lightning. Enter three Witches

FIRST WITCH

When shall we three meet again?
In thunder, lightning, or in rain?

SECOND WITCH

When the hurly-burly's done,
When the battle's lost and won.

THIRD WITCH

That will be ere the set of sun.

FIRST WITCH

Where the place?

SECOND WITCH   Upon the heath.

THIRD WITCH

There to meet with Macbeth.

FIRST WITCH

I come, Grey-Malkin.

SECOND WITCH   Padock calls!

THIRD WITCH   Anon!

ALL

Fair is foul, and foul is fair.
Hover through the fog and filthy air.   *Exeunt*   10

I.2   *Alarum within*
                Enter King Duncan, Malcolm, Donalbain, Lennox,
                with Attendants, meeting a bleeding Captain

KING
    What bloody man is that? He can report,
    As seemeth by his plight, of the revolt
    The newest state.
MALCOLM   This is the sergeant
    Who like a good and hardy soldier fought
    'Gainst my captivity. Hail, brave friend!
    Say to the King the knowledge of the broil
    As thou didst leave it.
CAPTAIN   Doubtful it stood,
    As two spent swimmers that do cling together
    And choke their art. The merciless Macdonwald –
10 Worthy to be a rebel, for to that
    The multiplying villainies of nature
    Do swarm upon him – from the Western Isles
    Of kerns and galloglasses is supplied,
    And fortune on his damnèd quarrel smiling
    Showed like a rebel's whore. But all's too weak:
    For brave Macbeth – well he deserves that name –
    Disdaining fortune, with his brandished steel,
    Which smoked with bloody execution,
    Like valour's minion carvèd out his passage
20 Till he faced the slave –
    Which ne'er shook hands nor bade farewell to him
    Till he unseamed him from the nave to the chops,
    And fixed his head upon our battlements.
KING
    O valiant cousin! Worthy gentleman!
CAPTAIN
    As, whence the sun 'gins his reflection,
    Shipwracking storms and direful thunders;

So, from that spring whence comfort seemed to come,
Discomfort swells. Mark, King of Scotland, mark!
No sooner justice had, with valour armed,
Compelled these skipping kerns to trust their heels   30
But the Norweyan lord, surveying vantage,
With furbished arms and new supplies of men,
Began a fresh assault.

KING   Dismayed not this
Our captains, Macbeth and Banquo?

CAPTAIN   Yes –
As sparrows, eagles, or the hare, the lion.
If I say sooth I must report they were
As cannons overcharged with double cracks;
So they
Doubly redoubled strokes upon the foe.
Except they meant to bathe in reeking wounds   40
Or memorize another Golgotha
I cannot tell.
– But I am faint; my gashes cry for help.

KING
So well thy words become thee as thy wounds,
They smack of honour both. Go get him surgeons.
                              Exit Captain with Attendants

    Enter Ross and Angus
Who comes here?

MALCOLM   The worthy Thane of Ross.

LENNOX
What a haste looks through his eyes!
So should he look that seems to speak things strange.

ROSS
God save the King!

KING
Whence cam'st thou, worthy thane?

ROSS   From Fife, great King,   50

Where the Norweyan banners flout the sky
And fan our people cold.
Norway himself, with terrible numbers,
Assisted by that most disloyal traitor,
The Thane of Cawdor, began a dismal conflict,
Till that Bellona's bridegroom, lapped in proof,
Confronted him with self-comparisons,
Point against point-rebellious, arm 'gainst arm,
Curbing his lavish spirit; and to conclude,

60   The victory fell on us —

KING   Great happiness!

ROSS

— That now Sweno, the Norways' king,
Craves composition;
Nor would we deign him burial of his men
Till he disbursèd at Saint Colm's Inch
Ten thousand dollars to our general use.

KING

No more that Thane of Cawdor shall deceive
Our bosom interest. Go pronounce his present death,
And with his former title greet Macbeth.

ROSS

I'll see it done.

KING

70   What he hath lost, noble Macbeth hath won.   *Exeunt*

I.3   *Thunder. Enter the three Witches*

FIRST WITCH Where hast thou been, sister?

SECOND WITCH Killing swine.

THIRD WITCH Sister, where thou?

FIRST WITCH

A sailor's wife had chestnuts in her lap,

And munched and munched and munched. 'Give me,'
    quoth I.
'Aroint thee, witch!' the rump-fed ronyon cries.
Her husband's to Aleppo gone, master o'the *Tiger*.
        But in a sieve I'll thither sail
        And like a rat without a tail
        I'll do, I'll do, and I'll do.   10

SECOND WITCH
        I'll give thee a wind.

FIRST WITCH
        Th'art kind.

THIRD WITCH
        And I another.

FIRST WITCH
        I myself have all the other.
        And the very ports they blow
        All the quarters that they know
        I'the shipman's card.
        I'll drain him dry as hay;
        Sleep shall neither night nor day
        Hang upon his penthouse lid.   20
        He shall live a man forbid.
        Weary sev'n-nights nine times nine
        Shall he dwindle, peak, and pine.
        Though his bark cannot be lost,
        Yet it shall be tempest-tossed.
        Look what I have!

SECOND WITCH   Show me, show me!

FIRST WITCH
        Here I have a pilot's thumb,
        Wracked as homeward he did come.

    Drum within

THIRD WITCH
        A drum! a drum!

30   Macbeth doth come.

ALL

          The Weird Sisters, hand in hand,
          Posters of the sea and land,
          Thus do go, about, about;
          Thrice to thine, and thrice to mine,
          And thrice again, to make up nine.
          Peace! The charm's wound up.
             Enter Macbeth and Banquo

MACBETH

     So foul and fair a day I have not seen.

BANQUO

     How far is't called to Forres? What are these,
     So withered and so wild in their attire,
40   That look not like the inhabitants o'the earth,
     And yet are on't? Live you? Or are you aught
     That man may question? You seem to understand me
     By each at once her choppy finger laying
     Upon her skinny lips. You should be women;
     And yet your beards forbid me to interpret
     That you are so.

MACBETH   Speak if you can! What are you?

FIRST WITCH

     All hail, Macbeth! Hail to thee, Thane of Glamis!

SECOND WITCH

     All hail, Macbeth! Hail to thee, Thane of Cawdor!

THIRD WITCH

     All hail, Macbeth, that shalt be king hereafter!

BANQUO

50   Good sir, why do you start, and seem to fear
     Things that do sound so fair? – I'the name of truth,
     Are ye fantastical, or that indeed
     Which outwardly ye show? My noble partner

You greet with present grace, and great prediction
Of noble having and of royal hope
That he seems rapt withal. To me you speak not.
If you can look into the seeds of time
And say which grain will grow and which will not,
Speak then to me who neither beg nor fear
Your favours nor your hate.   60

FIRST WITCH
Hail!

SECOND WITCH
Hail!

THIRD WITCH
Hail!

FIRST WITCH
Lesser than Macbeth, and greater.

SECOND WITCH
Not so happy, yet much happier.

THIRD WITCH
Thou shalt get kings, though thou be none.
So all hail, Macbeth and Banquo!

FIRST WITCH
Banquo and Macbeth, all hail!

MACBETH
Stay, you imperfect speakers! Tell me more!
By Sinell's death I know I am Thane of Glamis;   70
But how of Cawdor? The Thane of Cawdor lives
A prosperous gentleman. And to be king
Stands not within the prospect of belief –
No more than to be Cawdor. Say from whence
You owe this strange intelligence; or why
Upon this blasted heath you stop our way
With such prophetic greeting? Speak, I charge you!
                                        Witches vanish

BANQUO

    The earth hath bubbles as the water has,
    And these are of them. Whither are they vanished?

MACBETH

80   Into the air; and what seemed corporal
    Melted, as breath into the wind. Would they had stayed!

BANQUO

    Were such things here as we do speak about?
    Or have we eaten on the insane root
    That takes the reason prisoner?

MACBETH

    Your children shall be kings.

BANQUO   You shall be king.

MACBETH

    And Thane of Cawdor too, went it not so?

BANQUO

    To the selfsame tune and words. Who's here?

    Enter Ross and Angus

ROSS

    The King hath happily received, Macbeth,
    The news of thy success; and when he reads
90   Thy personal venture in the rebels' fight
    His wonders and his praises do contend
    Which should be thine, or his. Silenced with that,
    In viewing o'er the rest o'the selfsame day
    He finds thee in the stout Norweyan ranks,
    Nothing afeard of what thyself didst make,
    Strange images of death. As thick as hail
    Came post with post; and every one did bear
    Thy praises, in his kingdom's great defence,
    And poured them down before him.

ANGUS   We are sent
100   To give thee from our royal master thanks;

Only to herald thee into his sight,
Not pay thee.

ROSS

And, for an earnest of a greater honour,
He bade me from him call thee Thane of Cawdor
In which addition, hail, most worthy thane,
For it is thine.

BANQUO   What! Can the devil speak true?

MACBETH

The Thane of Cawdor lives. Why do you dress me
In borrowed robes?

ANGUS   Who was the Thane lives yet;
But under heavy judgement bears that life
Which he deserves to lose. Whether he was combined   110
With those of Norway, or did line the rebel
With hidden help and vantage, or that with both
He laboured in his country's wrack, I know not;
But treasons capital, confessed, and proved
Have overthrown him.

MACBETH (*aside*)   Glamis, and Thane of Cawdor!
The greatest is behind. – Thanks for your pains.
(*To Banquo*) Do you not hope your children shall be
      kings,
When those that gave the Thane of Cawdor to me
Promised no less to them?

BANQUO   That trusted home
Might yet enkindle you unto the crown   120
Besides the Thane of Cawdor. But 'tis strange;
And oftentimes, to win us to our harm,
The instruments of darkness tell us truths;
Win us with honest trifles, to betray's
In deepest consequence.
Cousins, a word, I pray you.
      They walk apart

MACBETH (*aside*)   Two truths are told
   As happy prologues to the swelling Act
   Of the imperial theme. – I thank you, gentlemen.
   (*Aside*) This supernatural soliciting
130 Cannot be ill, cannot be good. If ill,
   Why hath it given me earnest of success
   Commencing in a truth? I am Thane of Cawdor.
   If good, why do I yield to that suggestion
   Whose horrid image doth unfix my hair,
   And make my seated heart knock at my ribs
   Against the use of nature? Present fears
   Are less than horrible imaginings.
   My thought, whose murder yet is but fantastical,
   Shakes so my single state of man
140 That function is smothered in surmise,
   And nothing is but what is not.
BANQUO Look how our partner's rapt.
MACBETH (*aside*)
   If chance will have me king, why chance may crown me
   Without my stir.
BANQUO   New honours come upon him
   Like our strange garments, cleave not to their mould
   But with the aid of use.
MACBETH (*aside*)   Come what come may,
   Time and the hour runs through the roughest day.
BANQUO
   Worthy Macbeth, we stay upon your leisure.
MACBETH
   Give me your favour. My dull brain was wrought
150 With things forgotten. Kind gentlemen, your pains
   Are registered where every day I turn
   The leaf to read them. Let us toward the King.
   (*To Banquo*) Think upon what hath chanced, and at more
     time,

The interim having weighed it, let us speak
Our free hearts each to other.

BANQUO   Very gladly.

MACBETH

Till then, enough! – Come, friends.   *Exeunt*

Flourish. Enter King Duncan, Lennox, Malcolm,   I.4
Donalbain, and Attendants

KING

Is execution done on Cawdor?
Are not those in commission yet returned?

MALCOLM

My liege,
They are not yet come back. But I have spoke
With one that saw him die, who did report
That very frankly he confessed his treasons,
Implored your highness' pardon, and set forth
A deep repentance. Nothing in his life
Became him like the leaving it. He died
As one that had been studied in his death   10
To throw away the dearest thing he owed
As 'twere a careless trifle.

KING   There's no art
To find the mind's construction in the face.
He was a gentleman on whom I built
An absolute trust.

Enter Macbeth, Banquo, Ross, and Angus
                    O worthiest cousin!
The sin of my ingratitude even now
Was heavy on me. Thou art so far before,
That swiftest wing of recompense is slow
To overtake thee. Would thou hadst less deserved,
That the proportion both of thanks and payment   20

Might have been mine. Only I have left to say,
'More is thy due than more than all can pay.'

MACBETH

The service and the loyalty I owe,
In doing it, pays itself. Your highness' part
Is to receive our duties; and our duties
Are to your throne and state, children and servants,
Which do but what they should by doing everything
Safe toward your love and honour.

KING   Welcome hither.
I have begun to plant thee, and will labour
30   To make thee full of growing. — Noble Banquo,
That hast no less deserved, nor must be known
No less to have done so, let me enfold thee
And hold thee to my heart.

BANQUO   There if I grow,
The harvest is your own.

KING   My plenteous joys,
Wanton in fulness, seek to hide themselves
In drops of sorrow. Sons, kinsmen, thanes,
And you whose places are the nearest, know
We will establish our estate upon
Our eldest, Malcolm, whom we name hereafter
40   The Prince of Cumberland: which honour must
Not unaccompanied invest him only,
But signs of nobleness, like stars, shall shine
On all deservers. From hence to Inverness,
And bind us further to you.

MACBETH

The rest is labour, which is not used for you.
I'll be myself the harbinger and make joyful
The hearing of my wife with your approach;
So humbly take my leave.

KING   My worthy Cawdor!

MACBETH (aside)

    The Prince of Cumberland! That is a step
    On which I must fall down, or else o'erleap,   50
    For in my way it lies. Stars, hide your fires,
    Let not light see my black and deep desires.
    The eye wink at the hand; yet let that be
    Which the eye fears, when it is done, to see.   *Exit*

KING

    True, worthy Banquo; he is full so valiant,
    And in his commendations I am fed;
    It is a banquet to me. Let's after him
    Whose care is gone before to bid us welcome.
    It is a peerless kinsman.   *Flourish. Exeunt*

    Enter Macbeth's Wife alone with a letter   **I.5**

LADY *They met me in the day of success, and I have learned*
by the perfectest report they have more in them than mortal
knowledge. When I burned in desire to question them fur-
ther, they made themselves air, into which they vanished.
Whiles I stood rapt in the wonder of it, came missives from
the King, who all-hailed me Thane of Cawdor; by which
title before these Weird Sisters saluted me, and referred me
to the coming on of time with, 'Hail, king that shalt be.'
This have I thought good to deliver thee, my dearest partner
of greatness, that thou mightest not lose the dues of re-   10
joicing by being ignorant of what greatness is promised thee.
Lay it to thy heart, and farewell.

    Glamis thou art, and Cawdor, and shalt be
    What thou art promised. Yet do I fear thy nature:
    It is too full o'the milk of human-kindness
    To catch the nearest way. Thou wouldst be great,
    Art not without ambition, but without
    The illness should attend it. What thou wouldst highly

That wouldst thou holily, wouldst not play false,
20 And yet wouldst wrongly win. Thou'dst have, great
     Glamis,
That which cries, 'Thus thou must do' if thou have it,
And that which rather thou dost fear to do
Than wishest should be undone. Hie thee hither
That I may pour my spirits in thine ear,
And chastise with the valour of my tongue
All that impedes thee from the golden round
Which fate and metaphysical aid doth seem
To have thee crowned withal.

    Enter Messenger
                        What is your tidings?
MESSENGER
  The King comes here tonight.
LADY   Thou'rt mad to say it!
30 Is not thy master with him? Who, were't so,
  Would have informed for preparation.
MESSENGER
  So please you, it is true. Our Thane is coming;
  One of my fellows had the speed of him,
  Who, almost dead for breath, had scarcely more
  Than would make up his message.
LADY   Give him tending:
  He brings great news.   *Exit Messenger*
                 The raven himself is hoarse
That croaks the fatal entrance of Duncan
Under my battlements. Come, you spirits
That tend on mortal thoughts, unsex me here
40 And fill me from the crown to the toe top-full
Of direst cruelty. Make thick my blood;
Stop up the access and passage to remorse,
That no compunctious visitings of nature
Shake my fell purpose, nor keep peace between
The effect and it. Come to my woman's breasts

And take my milk for gall, you murdering ministers,
Wherever, in your sightless substances,
You wait on nature's mischief. Come, thick night,
And pall thee in the dunnest smoke of hell,
That my keen knife see not the wound it makes,   50
Nor heaven peep through the blanket of the dark
To cry, 'Hold, hold!'
   Enter Macbeth

               Great Glamis, worthy Cawdor!
Greater than both by the all-hail hereafter!
Thy letters have transported me beyond
This ignorant present, and I feel now
The future in the instant.

MACBETH   My dearest love,
Duncan comes here tonight.

LADY   And when goes hence?

MACBETH
Tomorrow, as he purposes.

LADY   O never
Shall sun that morrow see!
Your face, my thane, is as a book where men   60
May read strange matters. To beguile the time
Look like the time, bear welcome in your eye,
Your hand, your tongue; look like the innocent flower,
But be the serpent under't. He that's coming
Must be provided for; and you shall put
This night's great business into my dispatch,
Which shall to all our nights and days to come
Give solely sovereign sway and masterdom.

MACBETH
We will speak further.

LADY   Only look up clear:
To alter favour ever is to fear.   70
Leave all the rest to me.   *Exeunt*

1.6   *Hautboys and torches. Enter King Duncan,*
           Malcolm, Donalbain, Banquo, Lennox, Macduff,
           Ross, Angus, and Attendants

KING

   This castle hath a pleasant seat; the air
   Nimbly and sweetly recommends itself
   Unto our gentle senses.

BANQUO   This guest of summer,
   The temple-haunting martlet, does approve
   By his loved mansionry that the heaven's breath
   Smells wooingly here; no jutty, frieze,
   Buttress, nor coign of vantage, but this bird
   Hath made his pendent bed and procreant cradle;
   Where they most breed and haunt I have observed
10 The air is delicate.

           Enter Lady Macbeth

KING   See, see, our honoured hostess —
   The love that follows us sometime is our trouble,
   Which still we thank as love. Herein I teach you
   How you shall bid 'God 'ield us' for your pains,
   And thank us for your trouble.

LADY   All our service
   In every point twice done and then done double
   Were poor and single business to contend
   Against those honours deep and broad wherewith
   Your majesty loads our house. For those of old,
   And the late dignities heaped up to them,
20 We rest your hermits.

KING   Where's the Thane of Cawdor?
   We coursed him at the heels and had a purpose
   To be his purveyor; but he rides well,
   And his great love, sharp as his spur, hath holp him
   To his home before us. Fair and noble hostess,
   We are your guest tonight.

LADY   Your servants ever
  Have theirs, themselves, and what is theirs, in compt,
  To make their audit at your highness' pleasure,
  Still to return your own.
KING   Give me your hand;
  Conduct me to mine host. We love him highly,
  And shall continue our graces towards him.   30
  By your leave, hostess.   *He kisses her. Exeunt*

    Hautboys. Torches. Enter a Sewer and divers   I.7
    Servants with dishes and service over the stage.
    Then enter Macbeth
MACBETH
  If it were done when 'tis done, then 'twere well
  It were done quickly. If the assassination
  Could trammel up the consequence, and catch
  With his surcease success – that but this blow
  Might be the be-all and the end-all! – here,
  But here, upon this bank and shoal of time,
  We'd jump the life to come. But in these cases
  We still have judgement here – that we but teach
  Bloody instructions, which, being taught, return
  To plague the inventor. This even-handed justice   10
  Commends the ingredience of our poisoned chalice
  To our own lips. He's here in double trust:
  First, as I am his kinsman and his subject,
  Strong both against the deed; then, as his host,
  Who should against his murderer shut the door,
  Not bear the knife myself. Besides, this Duncan
  Hath borne his faculties so meek, hath been
  So clear in his great office, that his virtues
  Will plead like angels, trumpet-tongued against
  The deep damnation of his taking-off;   20

And Pity, like a naked new-born babe
Striding the blast, or heaven's cherubin, horsed
Upon the sightless curriers of the air,
Shall blow the horrid deed in every eye,
That tears shall drown the wind. I have no spur
To prick the sides of my intent but only
Vaulting ambition which o'erleaps itself
And falls on the other.

    Enter Lady Macbeth

                    How now? What news?

LADY

He has almost supped. Why have you left the chamber?

MACBETH

30   Hath he asked for me?

LADY   Know you not he has?

MACBETH

We will proceed no further in this business.
He hath honoured me of late, and I have bought
Golden opinions from all sorts of people
Which would be worn now in their newest gloss,
Not cast aside so soon.

LADY   Was the hope drunk
Wherein you dressed yourself? Hath it slept since?
And wakes it now to look so green and pale
At what it did so freely? From this time
Such I account thy love. Art thou afeard

40   To be the same in thine own act and valour
As thou art in desire? Wouldst thou have that
Which thou esteem'st the ornament of life,
And live a coward in thine own esteem,
Letting 'I dare not' wait upon 'I would',
Like the poor cat i'the adage?

MACBETH   Prithee peace.
I dare do all that may become a man;

Who dares do more is none.

LADY   What beast was't then
That made you break this enterprise to me?
When you durst do it, then you were a man;
And to be more than what you were, you would   50
Be so much more the man. Nor time nor place
Did then adhere, and yet you would make both.
They have made themselves, and that their fitness now
Does unmake you. I have given suck, and know
How tender 'tis to love the babe that milks me;
I would while it was smiling in my face
Have plucked my nipple from his boneless gums
And dashed the brains out, had I so sworn as you
Have done to this.

MACBETH   If we should fail?

LADY   We fail!
But screw your courage to the sticking place,   60
And we'll not fail. When Duncan is asleep –
Whereto the rather shall his day's hard journey
Soundly invite him – his two chamberlains
Will I with wine and wassail so convince
That memory, the warder of the brain,
Shall be a-fume, and the receipt of reason
A limbeck only. When in swinish sleep
Their drenchèd natures lies as in a death,
What cannot you and I perform upon
The unguarded Duncan? What not put upon   70
His spongy officers, who shall bear the guilt
Of our great quell?

MACBETH   Bring forth men-children only!
For thy undaunted mettle should compose
Nothing but males. Will it not be received,
When we have marked with blood those sleepy two
Of his own chamber, and used their very daggers,

That they have done't?

LADY   Who dares receive it other,
As we shall make our griefs and clamour roar
Upon his death?

MACBETH   I am settled; and bend up
80   Each corporal agent to this terrible feat.
Away, and mock the time with fairest show:
False face must hide what the false heart doth know.

                                                        Exeunt

                                *

II.I   *Enter Banquo, and Fleance with a torch before him*

BANQUO
How goes the night, boy?

FLEANCE
The moon is down; I have not heard the clock.

BANQUO
And she goes down at twelve.

FLEANCE   I take't 'tis later, sir.

BANQUO
Hold, take my sword. There's husbandry in heaven:
Their candles are all out. Take thee that too.
A heavy summons lies like lead upon me
And yet I would not sleep. Merciful powers,
Restrain in me the cursèd thoughts that nature
Gives way to in repose.
          Enter Macbeth and a Servant with a torch
                              Give me my sword!
10   Who's there?

MACBETH
A friend.

BANQUO

 What, sir, not yet at rest? The King's a-bed.

 He hath been in unusual pleasure,

 And sent forth great largess to your offices.

 This diamond he greets your wife withal

 By the name of most kind hostess, and shut up

 In measureless content.

MACBETH   Being unprepared

 Our will became the servant to defect,

 Which else should free have wrought.

BANQUO   All's well.

 I dreamt last night of the three Weird Sisters.   20

 To you they have showed some truth.

MACBETH   I think not of them.

 Yet, when we can entreat an hour to serve,

 We would spend it in some words upon that business,

 If you would grant the time.

BANQUO   At your kind'st leisure.

MACBETH

 If you shall cleave to my consent when 'tis,

 It shall make honour for you.

BANQUO   So I lose none

 In seeking to augment it, but still keep

 My bosom franchised and allegiance clear,

 I shall be counselled.

MACBETH   Good repose the while.

BANQUO

 Thanks, sir; the like to you.   *Exit Banquo and Fleance*   30

MACBETH

 Go bid thy mistress, when my drink is ready

 She strike upon the bell. Get thee to bed.

              Exit Servant

 Is this a dagger which I see before me,

The handle toward my hand? Come, let me clutch thee –
I have thee not and yet I see thee still!
Art thou not, fatal vision, sensible
To feeling as to sight? Or art thou but
A dagger of the mind, a false creation,
Proceeding from the heat-oppressèd brain?
40   I see thee yet, in form as palpable
As this which now I draw.
Thou marshall'st me the way that I was going,
And such an instrument I was to use. –
Mine eyes are made the fools o'the other senses,
Or else worth all the rest. – I see thee still;
And, on thy blade and dudgeon, gouts of blood,
Which was not so before. There's no such thing.
It is the bloody business which informs
Thus to mine eyes. Now o'er the one half-world
50   Nature seems dead, and wicked dreams abuse
The curtained sleep. Witchcraft celebrates
Pale Hecat's offerings; and withered Murder,
Alarumed by his sentinel the wolf,
Whose howl's his watch, thus with his stealthy pace,
With Tarquin's ravishing strides, towards his design
Moves like a ghost. Thou sure and firm-set earth,
Hear not my steps, which way they walk, for fear
Thy very stones prate of my whereabout
And take the present horror from the time
60   Which now suits with it. – Whiles I threat, he lives:
Words to the heat of deeds too cold breath gives.
       A bell rings
I go, and it is done; the bell invites me.
Hear it not, Duncan, for it is a knell
That summons thee to heaven or to hell.   *Exit*

Enter Lady Macbeth

LADY

That which hath made them drunk hath made me bold;
What hath quenched them hath given me fire. – Hark! –
      Peace!
It was the owl that shrieked, the fatal bellman
Which gives the stern'st good-night. He is about it.
The doors are open, and the surfeited grooms
Do mock their charge with snores; I have drugged their
      possets
That death and nature do contend about them
Whether they live or die.

MACBETH (*within*)   Who's there? What, ho!

LADY

Alack, I am afraid they have awaked,
And 'tis not done. The attempt and not the deed   10
Confounds us. – Hark! – I laid their daggers ready;
He could not miss 'em. Had he not resembled
My father as he slept, I had done 't.
      Enter Macbeth, carrying two bloodstained daggers
                                    My husband!

MACBETH

I have done the deed. Didst thou not hear a noise?

LADY

I heard the owl-scream and the cricket's cry.
Did not you speak?

MACBETH   When?

LADY   Now.

MACBETH   As I descended?

LADY

Ay.

MACBETH

Hark!

Who lies i'the second chamber?

LADY   Donalbain.

MACBETH (*looks at his hands*)

20 This is a sorry sight.

LADY

A foolish thought, to say a sorry sight.

MACBETH

There's one did laugh in's sleep, and one cried 'Murder!'
That they did wake each other. I stood and heard them.
But they did say their prayers and addressed them
Again to sleep.

LADY   There are two lodged together.

MACBETH

One cried 'God bless us' and 'Amen' the other,
As they had seen me with these hangman's hands.
Listening their fear I could not say 'Amen'
When they did say 'God bless us.'

LADY

30 Consider it not so deeply.

MACBETH

But wherefore could not I pronounce 'Amen'?
I had most need of blessing, and 'Amen'
Stuck in my throat.

LADY   These deeds must not be thought
After these ways; so, it will make us mad.

MACBETH

Methought I heard a voice cry, 'Sleep no more!
Macbeth does murder sleep – the innocent sleep,
Sleep that knits up the ravelled sleave of care,
The death of each day's life, sore labour's bath,
Balm of hurt minds, great nature's second course,
40 Chief nourisher in life's feast.'

LADY   What do you mean?

MACBETH

Still it cried 'Sleep no more' to all the house;
'Glamis hath murdered sleep, and therefore Cawdor
Shall sleep no more, Macbeth shall sleep no more.'

LADY

Who was it that thus cried? Why, worthy thane,
You do unbend your noble strength, to think
So brain-sickly of things. Go, get some water,
And wash this filthy witness from your hand.
Why did you bring these daggers from the place?
They must lie there. Go, carry them and smear
The sleepy grooms with blood.

MACBETH   I'll go no more.   50
I am afraid to think what I have done;
Look on't again I dare not.

LADY   Infirm of purpose!
Give me the daggers. The sleeping and the dead
Are but as pictures. 'Tis the eye of childhood
That fears a painted devil. If he do bleed,
I'll gild the faces of the grooms withal,
For it must seem their guilt.   *Exit*

  Knock within

MACBETH   Whence is that knocking?
How is't with me when every noise appals me?
What hands are here! Ha – they pluck out mine eyes!
Will all great Neptune's ocean wash this blood   60
Clean from my hand? No, this my hand will rather
The multitudinous seas incarnadine,
Making the green one red.

  Enter Lady Macbeth

LADY

My hands are of your colour; but I shame
To wear a heart so white.

  Knock

                              I hear a knocking
At the south entry. Retire we to our chamber.
A little water clears us of this deed;
How easy is it then! Your constancy
Hath left you unattended.
          Knock

                              Hark! more knocking.
70   Get on your nightgown, lest occasion call us
      And show us to be watchers. Be not lost
      So poorly in your thoughts.
MACBETH
      To know my deed 'twere best not know myself.
          Knock
      Wake Duncan with thy knocking! I would thou couldst!
                                                    Exeunt

II.3   *Enter a Porter. Knocking within*
      PORTER Here's a knocking indeed! If a man were porter of
      hell-gate he should have old turning the key.
          Knock
      Knock, knock, knock! Who's there i'the name of
      Belzebub? Here's a farmer that hanged himself on the
      expectation of plenty. Come in time! Have napkins enow
      about you; here you'll sweat for't.
          Knock
      Knock, knock! Who's there in the other devil's name?
      Faith, here's an equivocator that could swear in both the
      scales against either scale, who committed treason
10   enough for God's sake, yet could not equivocate to
      heaven. O, come in, equivocator.
          Knock
      Knock, knock, knock! Who's there? Faith, here's an
      English tailor come hither for stealing out of a French

hose. Come in, tailor; here you may roast your goose.

Knock

Knock, knock! Never at quiet! What are you? – But this
place is too cold for hell. I'll devil-porter it no further.
I had thought to have let in some of all professions that
go the primrose way to the everlasting bonfire.

Knock

Anon, anon! I pray you remember the porter.

He opens the gate. Enter Macduff and Lennox

MACDUFF

Was it so late, friend, ere you went to bed,   20
That you do lie so late?

PORTER Faith, sir, we were carousing till the second
cock; and drink, sir, is a great provoker of three things.

MACDUFF What three things does drink especially pro-
voke?

PORTER Marry, sir, nose-painting, sleep, and urine.
Lechery, sir, it provokes and unprovokes: it provokes
the desire but it takes away the performance. Therefore
much drink may be said to be an equivocator with
lechery: it makes him and it mars him; it sets him on and   30
it takes him off; it persuades him and disheartens him,
makes him stand to and not stand to; in conclusion, equivocates him in a sleep and giving him the lie, leaves him.

MACDUFF I believe drink gave thee the lie last night.

PORTER That it did, sir, i'the very throat on me. But I
requited him for his lie and, I think, being too strong
for him, though he took up my legs sometime, yet I
made a shift to cast him.

MACDUFF Is thy master stirring?

Enter Macbeth

Our knocking has awaked him; here he comes.   40

LENNOX

Good morrow, noble sir.

MACBETH   Good morrow both.

MACDUFF

Is the King stirring, worthy thane?

MACBETH   Not yet.

MACDUFF

He did command me to call timely on him.

I have almost slipped the hour.

MACBETH   I'll bring you to him.

MACDUFF

I know this is a joyful trouble to you,

But yet 'tis one.

MACBETH

The labour we delight in physics pain.

This is the door.

MACDUFF   I'll make so bold to call,

For 'tis my limited service.   *Exit*

LENNOX

50 Goes the King hence today?

MACBETH   He does; he did appoint so.

LENNOX

The night has been unruly. Where we lay,

Our chimneys were blown down, and, as they say,

Lamentings heard i'the air, strange screams of death,

And prophesying, with accents terrible,

Of dire combustion and confused events

New-hatched to the woeful time. The obscure bird

Clamoured the live-long night. Some say the earth

Was feverous and did shake.

MACBETH   'Twas a rough night.

LENNOX

My young remembrance cannot parallel

60 A fellow to it.

    Enter Macduff

MACDUFF   O horror, horror, horror!

Tongue nor heart cannot conceive nor name thee!

MACBETH *and* LENNOX

What's the matter?

MACDUFF

Confusion now hath made his masterpiece;
Most sacrilegious murder hath broke ope
The Lord's anointed temple and stole thence
The life o'the building.

MACBETH   What is't you say? The life?

LENNOX

Mean you his majesty?

MACDUFF

Approach the chamber and destroy your sight
With a new Gorgon. Do not bid me speak.
See, and then speak yourselves.

Exeunt Macbeth and Lennox

Awake, awake!   70
Ring the alarum bell! Murder and treason!
Banquo and Donalbain, Malcolm, awake!
Shake off this downy sleep, death's counterfeit,
And look on death itself! Up, up, and see
The Great Doom's image! Malcolm, Banquo,
As from your graves rise up and walk like sprites
To countenance this horror. Ring the bell!

  Bell rings
  Enter Lady Macbeth

LADY

What's the business,
That such a hideous trumpet calls to parley
The sleepers of the house? Speak, speak!

MACDUFF   O gentle lady,   80
'Tis not for you to hear what I can speak.
The repetition in a woman's ear
Would murder as it fell.

Enter Banquo

                           O Banquo, Banquo!
Our royal master's murdered.

LADY   Woe, alas!
What, in our house!

BANQUO   Too cruel, anywhere.
Dear Duff, I prithee contradict thyself
And say it is not so.

    Enter Macbeth, Lennox, and Ross

MACBETH

Had I but died an hour before this chance
I had lived a blessèd time; for from this instant
There's nothing serious in mortality.
All is but toys, renown and grace is dead,
The wine of life is drawn, and the mere lees
Is left this vault to brag of.

    Enter Malcolm and Donalbain

DONALBAIN

What is amiss?

MACBETH   You are, and do not know't.
The spring, the head, the fountain of your blood
Is stopped, the very source of it is stopped.

MACDUFF

Your royal father's murdered.

MALCOLM   O, by whom?

LENNOX

Those of his chamber, as it seemed, had done't:
Their hands and faces were all badged with blood,
So were their daggers, which, unwiped, we found
Upon their pillows; they stared and were distracted;
No man's life was to be trusted with them.

MACBETH

O yet I do repent me of my fury,
That I did kill them.

MACDUFF   Wherefore did you so?
MACBETH
  Who can be wise, amazed, temperate and furious,
  Loyal and neutral, in a moment? No man.
  The expedition of my violent love
  Outrun the pauser reason. Here lay Duncan,
  His silver skin laced with his golden blood,
  And his gashed stabs looked like a breach in nature   110
  For ruin's wasteful entrance; there the murderers,
  Steeped in the colours of their trade, their daggers
  Unmannerly breeched with gore. Who could refrain,
  That had a heart to love, and in that heart
  Courage to make's love known?
LADY (*swooning*)   Help me hence, ho!
MACDUFF
  Look to the lady!
MALCOLM (*to Donalbain*) Why do we hold our tongues,
  That most may claim this argument for ours?
DONALBAIN (*to Malcolm*)
  What should be spoken here where our fate,
  Hid in an auger-hole, may rush and seize us?
  Let's away. Our tears are not yet brewed.   120
MALCOLM (*to Donalbain*)
  Nor our strong sorrow upon the foot of motion.
BANQUO
  Look to the lady!
    Lady Macbeth is taken out
  And when we have our naked frailties hid
  That suffer in exposure, let us meet
  And question this most bloody piece of work
  To know it further. Fears and scruples shake us.
  In the great hand of God I stand, and thence
  Against the undivulged pretence I fight
  Of treasonous malice.

MACDUFF   And so do I.

ALL   So all.

MACBETH

130 Let's briefly put on manly readiness,
     And meet i'the hall together.

ALL   Well contented.

Exeunt all but Malcolm and Donalbain

MALCOLM

What will you do? Let's not consort with them.
To show an unfelt sorrow is an office
Which the false man does easy. I'll to England.

DONALBAIN

To Ireland, I. Our separated fortune
Shall keep us both the safer. Where we are
There's daggers in men's smiles. The nea'er in blood
The nearer bloody.

MALCOLM   This murderous shaft that's shot
Hath not yet lighted; and our safest way

140 Is to avoid the aim. Therefore to horse,
     And let us not be dainty of leave-taking
     But shift away. There's warrant in that theft
     Which steals itself when there's no mercy left. *Exeunt*

II.4   *Enter Ross with an Old Man*

OLD MAN

Threescore and ten I can remember well;
Within the volume of which time I have seen
Hours dreadful and things strange; but this sore night
Hath trifled former knowings.

ROSS   Ha, good father,
Thou seest the heavens, as troubled with man's act,
Threatens his bloody stage. By the clock 'tis day,
And yet dark night strangles the travelling lamp;

Is't night's predominance or the day's shame
That darkness does the face of earth entomb
When living light should kiss it?

OLD MAN   'Tis unnatural,   10
Even like the deed that's done. On Tuesday last,
A falcon towering in her pride of place
Was by a mousing owl hawked at and killed.

ROSS
And Duncan's horses — a thing most strange and cer-
        tain —
Beauteous and swift, the minions of their race,
Turned wild in nature, broke their stalls, flung out,
Contending 'gainst obedience, as they would
Make war with mankind.

OLD MAN   'Tis said they ate each other.

ROSS
They did so, to the amazement of mine eyes
That looked upon't.

    Enter Macduff

                        Here comes the good Macduff.   20
How goes the world, sir, now?

MACDUFF   Why, see you not?

ROSS
Is't known who did this more than bloody deed?

MACDUFF
Those that Macbeth hath slain.

ROSS   Alas the day!
What good could they pretend?

MACDUFF   They were suborned.
Malcolm and Donalbain, the King's two sons,
Are stolen away and fled, which puts upon them
Suspicion of the deed.

ROSS   'Gainst nature still!
Thriftless ambition that will raven up

Thine own life's means! – Then 'tis most like
30   The sovereignty will fall upon Macbeth?

MACDUFF

He is already named and gone to Scone
To be invested.

ROSS   Where is Duncan's body?

MACDUFF

Carried to Colmekill,
The sacred storehouse of his predecessors
And guardian of their bones.

ROSS   Will you to Scone?

MACDUFF

No, cousin, I'll to Fife.

ROSS   Well, I will thither.

MACDUFF

Well, may you see things well done there – Adieu! –
Lest our old robes sit easier than our new.

ROSS

Farewell, father.

OLD MAN

40   God's benison go with you, and with those
That would make good of bad, and friends of foes!

                                      Exeunt

*

III.I   *Enter Banquo*

BANQUO

Thou hast it now: King, Cawdor, Glamis, all
As the weird women promised; and I fear
Thou playedst most foully for't. Yet it was said
It should not stand in thy posterity
But that myself should be the root and father

Of many kings. If there come truth from them,
As upon thee, Macbeth, their speeches shine,
Why by the verities on thee made good
May they not be my oracles as well
And set me up in hope? But hush! No more.   10
    Sennet sounded. Enter Macbeth as King, Lady Mac-
    beth, Lennox, Ross, Lords, and Attendants

MACBETH
Here's our chief guest.

LADY   If he had been forgotten
It had been as a gap in our great feast
And all-thing unbecoming.

MACBETH
Tonight we hold a solemn supper, sir,
And I'll request your presence.

BANQUO   Let your highness
Command upon me, to the which my duties
Are with a most indissoluble tie
Forever knit.

MACBETH
Ride you this afternoon?

BANQUO   Ay, my good lord.

MACBETH
We should have else desired your good advice,   20
Which still hath been both grave and prosperous,
In this day's council; but we'll take tomorrow.
Is't far you ride?

BANQUO
As far, my lord, as will fill up the time
'Twixt this and supper. Go not my horse the better,
I must become a borrower of the night
For a dark hour or twain.

MACBETH   Fail not our feast.

BANQUO
  My lord, I will not.
MACBETH
  We hear our bloody cousins are bestowed
30 In England and in Ireland, not confessing
  Their cruel parricide, filling their hearers
  With strange invention. But of that tomorrow,
  When therewithal we shall have cause of state
  Craving us jointly. Hie you to horse. Adieu
  Till you return at night. Goes Fleance with you?
BANQUO
  Ay, my good lord; our time does call upon's.
MACBETH
  I wish your horses swift and sure of foot;
  And so I do commend you to their backs.
  Farewell.   *Exit Banquo*
40 Let every man be master of his time
  Till seven at night.
  To make society the sweeter welcome,
  We will keep ourself till supper-time alone.
  While then, God be with you!
                          Exeunt Lords and Lady Macbeth
                  Sirrah!
  A word with you. Attend those men our pleasure?
SERVANT
  They are, my lord, without the palace gate.
MACBETH
  Bring them before us.   *Exit Servant*
                  To be thus is nothing;
  But to be safely thus! – Our fears in Banquo
  Stick deep; and in his royalty of nature
50 Reigns that which would be feared. 'Tis much he dares,
  And to that dauntless temper of his mind
  He hath a wisdom that doth guide his valour

To act in safety. There is none but he
Whose being I do fear; and under him
My genius is rebuked as, it is said,
Mark Antony's was by Caesar. He chid the sisters
When first they put the name of king upon me,
And bade them speak to him. Then, prophet-like,
They hailed him father to a line of kings.
Upon my head they placed a fruitless crown   60
And put a barren sceptre in my grip,
Thence to be wrenched with an unlineal hand,
No son of mine succeeding. If it be so,
For Banquo's issue have I filed my mind,
For them the gracious Duncan have I murdered,
Put rancours in the vessel of my peace,
Only for them; and mine eternal jewel
Given to the common enemy of man,
To make them kings, the seeds of Banquo kings!
Rather than so, come fate into the list   70
And champion me to the utterance! Who's there?
    Enter Servant and two Murderers
Now go to the door, and stay there till we call.
                                        Exit Servant
Was it not yesterday we spoke together?

MURDERERS

It was, so please your highness.

MACBETH   Well then now,
Have you considered of my speeches? Know
That it was he in the times past which held you
So under fortune, which you thought had been
Our innocent self. This I made good to you
In our last conference; passed in probation with you
How you were borne in hand, how crossed, the
        instruments,   80
Who wrought with them, and all things else that might

To half a soul and to a notion crazed
Say, 'Thus did Banquo.'

FIRST MURDERER   You made it known to us.

MACBETH

I did so; and went further, which is now
Our point of second meeting. Do you find
Your patience so predominant in your nature
That you can let this go? Are you so gospelled,
To pray for this good man and for his issue,
Whose heavy hand hath bowed you to the grave,
90   And beggared yours for ever?

FIRST MURDERER   We are men, my liege.

MACBETH

Ay, in the catalogue ye go for men,
As hounds and greyhounds, mongrels, spaniels, curs,
Shoughs, water-rugs, and demi-wolves are clept
All by the name of dogs. The valued file
Distinguishes the swift, the slow, the subtle,
The house-keeper, the hunter, every one
According to the gift which bounteous nature
Hath in him closed; whereby he does receive
Particular addition from the bill
100   That writes them all alike. And so of men.
Now, if you have a station in the file,
Not i'the worst rank of manhood, say't,
And I will put that business in your bosoms,
Whose execution takes your enemy off,
Grapples you to the heart and love of us,
Who wear our health but sickly in his life,
Which in his death were perfect.

SECOND MURDERER   I am one, my liege,
Whom the vile blows and buffets of the world
Hath so incensed that I am reckless what I do
110   To spite the world.

FIRST MURDERER   And I another,
  So weary with disasters, tugged with fortune,
  That I would set my life on any chance
  To mend it or be rid on't.
MACBETH   Both of you
  Know Banquo was your enemy.
MURDERERS   True, my lord.
MACBETH
  So is he mine, and in such bloody distance
  That every minute of his being thrusts
  Against my near'st of life; and though I could
  With bare-faced power sweep him from my sight
  And bid my will avouch it, yet I must not,
  For certain friends that are both his and mine,   120
  Whose loves I may not drop, but wail his fall
  Who I myself struck down. And thence it is
  That I to your assistance do make love,
  Masking the business from the common eye
  For sundry weighty reasons.
SECOND MURDERER   We shall, my lord,
  Perform what you command us.
FIRST MURDERER   Though our lives –
MACBETH
  Your spirits shine through you. Within this hour, at most,
  I will advise you where to plant yourselves,
  Acquaint you with the perfect spy o'the time,
  The moment on't; for't must be done tonight;   130
  And something from the palace; always thought
  That I require a clearness; and with him,
  To leave no rubs nor botches in the work,
  Fleance his son, that keeps him company,
  Whose absence is no less material to me
  Than is his father's, must embrace the fate
  Of that dark hour. Resolve yourselves apart;

I'll come to you anon.

MURDERERS   We are resolved, my lord.

MACBETH

I'll call upon you straight. Abide within.

Exeunt Murderers

140   It is concluded! Banquo, thy soul's flight,
       If it find heaven, must find it out tonight.   *Exit*

III.2   *Enter Macbeth's Lady and a Servant*

LADY

Is Banquo gone from court?

SERVANT

Ay, madam, but returns again tonight.

LADY

Say to the King I would attend his leisure
For a few words.

SERVANT   Madam, I will.   *Exit*

LADY   Naught's had, all's spent,
Where our desire is got without content.
'Tis safer to be that which we destroy
Than by destruction dwell in doubtful joy.

       Enter Macbeth

How now, my lord? Why do you keep alone,
Of sorriest fancies your companions making,
10   Using those thoughts which should indeed have died
With them they think on? Things without all remedy
Should be without regard; what's done is done.

MACBETH

We have scorched the snake, not killed it;
She'll close and be herself, whilst our poor malice
Remains in danger of her former tooth.
But let the frame of things disjoint, both the worlds suffer
Ere we will eat our meal in fear, and sleep

In the affliction of these terrible dreams
That shake us nightly; better be with the dead
Whom we, to gain our peace, have sent to peace,   20
Than on the torture of the mind to lie
In restless ecstasy. Duncan is in his grave;
After life's fitful fever he sleeps well;
Treason has done his worst. Nor steel, nor poison,
Malice domestic, foreign levy, nothing
Can touch him further.

LADY   Come on,
Gentle my lord, sleek o'er your rugged looks,
Be bright and jovial among your guests tonight.

MACBETH
So shall I, love; and so I pray be you.
Let your remembrance apply to Banquo,   30
Present him eminence both with eye and tongue.
Unsafe the while that we
Must lave our honours in these flattering streams,
And make our faces vizards to our hearts,
Disguising what they are.

LADY   You must leave this.

MACBETH
O, full of scorpions is my mind, dear wife!
Thou know'st that Banquo and his Fleance lives.

LADY
But in them nature's copy's not eterne.

MACBETH
There's comfort yet! They are assailable.
Then be thou jocund. Ere the bat hath flown   40
His cloistered flight, ere to black Hecat's summons
The shard-borne beetle, with his drowsy hums,
Hath rung night's yawning peal, there shall be done
A deed of dreadful note.

LADY   What's to be done?

MACBETH
>Be innocent of the knowledge, dearest chuck,
>Till thou applaud the deed. Come, seeling night,
>Scarf up the tender eye of pitiful day,
>And with thy bloody and invisible hand
>Cancel and tear to pieces that great bond
>Which keeps me pale. Light thickens
>And the crow makes wing to the rooky wood;
>Good things of day begin to droop and drowse,
>Whiles night's black agents to their preys do rouse.
>Thou marvell'st at my words; but hold thee still.
>Things bad begun make strong themselves by ill.
>So, prithee, go with me.   *Exeunt*

III.3   *Enter three Murderers*

FIRST MURDERER
>But who did bid thee join with us?

THIRD MURDERER   Macbeth.

SECOND MURDERER
>He needs not our mistrust, since he delivers
>Our offices and what we have to do
>To the direction just.

FIRST MURDERER   Then stand with us;
>The west yet glimmers with some streaks of day.
>Now spurs the lated traveller apace
>To gain the timely inn; and near approaches
>The subject of our watch.

THIRD MURDERER   Hark, I hear horses!

BANQUO (*within*)
>Give us a light there, ho!

SECOND MURDERER   Then 'tis he.
>The rest that are within the note of expectation,
>Already are i'the court.

FIRST MURDERER   His horses go about.

THIRD MURDERER

Almost a mile; but he does usually.
So all men do, from hence to the palace gate
Make it their walk.

  Enter Banquo and Fleance, with a torch

SECOND MURDERER

A light, a light!

THIRD MURDERER

                'Tis he.

FIRST MURDERER   Stand to't!

BANQUO

It will be rain tonight.

FIRST MURDERER   Let it come down!

  They attack Banquo

BANQUO

O treachery! Fly, good Fleance, fly, fly, fly!
Thou mayst revenge – O slave!

  Banquo falls. Fleance escapes

THIRD MURDERER

Who did strike out the light?

FIRST MURDERER   Was't not the way?

THIRD MURDERER

There's but one down; the son is fled.

SECOND MURDERER   We have lost   20
Best half of our affair.

FIRST MURDERER

Well, let's away and say how much is done.   *Exeunt*

  Banquet prepared. Enter Macbeth, Lady Macbeth,   III.4
  Ross, Lennox, Lords, and Attendants

MACBETH

You know your own degrees, sit down. At first

And last, the hearty welcome.

LORDS   Thanks to your majesty.

MACBETH

Ourself will mingle with society

And play the humble host.

   He walks around the tables

Our hostess keeps her state; but in best time

We will require her welcome.

LADY

Pronounce it for me, sir, to all our friends,

For my heart speaks they are welcome.

   Enter First Murderer

MACBETH

See, they encounter thee with their hearts' thanks;

10   Both sides are even. Here I'll sit i'the midst.

Be large in mirth. Anon we'll drink a measure

The table round.

   He rises and goes to the Murderer

There's blood upon thy face!

FIRST MURDERER   'Tis Banquo's then.

MACBETH

'Tis better thee without than he within.

Is he dispatched?

FIRST MURDERER My lord, his throat is cut;

That I did for him.

MACBETH   Thou art the best o'the cut-throats.

Yet he's good that did the like for Fleance.

If thou didst it, thou art the nonpareil.

FIRST MURDERER

Most royal sir – Fleance is scaped.

MACBETH

20   Then comes my fit again. I had else been perfect,

Whole as the marble, founded as the rock,

As broad and general as the casing air;

But now I am cabined, cribbed, confined, bound in
To saucy doubts and fears. – But Banquo's safe?

FIRST MURDERER

Ay, my good lord; safe in a ditch he bides,
With twenty trenchèd gashes on his head,
The least a death to nature.

MACBETH   Thanks for that.
There the grown serpent lies. The worm that's fled
Hath nature that in time will venom breed,
No teeth for the present. Get thee gone. Tomorrow   30
We'll hear ourselves again.   *Exit Murderer*

LADY   My royal lord,
You do not give the cheer. The feast is sold
That is not often vouched, while 'tis a-making,
'Tis given with welcome. To feed were best at home;
From thence, the sauce to meat is ceremony;
Meeting were bare without it.

MACBETH   Sweet remembrancer!
Now good digestion wait on appetite,
And health on both!

LENNOX   May't please your highness sit.
Enter the Ghost of Banquo and sits in Macbeth's place

MACBETH

Here had we now our country's honour roofed,
Were the graced person of our Banquo present;   40
Who may I rather challenge for unkindness
Than pity for mischance.

ROSS   His absence, sir,
Lays blame upon his promise. Please't your highness
To grace us with your royal company?

MACBETH

The table's full.

LENNOX   Here is a place reserved, sir.

MACBETH
  Where?

LENNOX
  Here, my good lord. What is't that moves your highness?

MACBETH
  Which of you have done this?

LORDS   What, my good lord?

MACBETH
  Thou canst not say I did it; never shake
50 Thy gory locks at me.

ROSS
  Gentlemen, rise. His highness is not well.

LADY (*descends from her throne*)
  Sit, worthy friends. My lord is often thus;
  And hath been from his youth. Pray you keep seat.
  The fit is momentary; upon a thought
  He will again be well. If much you note him,
  You shall offend him and extend his passion.
  Feed, and regard him not. – Are you a man?

MACBETH
  Ay, and a bold one, that dare look on that
  Which might appal the devil.

LADY   O proper stuff!
60 This is the very painting of your fear.
  This is the air-drawn dagger which you said
  Led you to Duncan. O, these flaws and starts,
  Impostors to true fear, would well become
  A woman's story at a winter's fire,
  Authorized by her grandam. Shame itself!
  Why do you make such faces? When all's done
  You look but on a stool.

MACBETH   Prithee, see there!
  Behold! Look! Lo! – How say you?
  Why, what care I if thou canst nod! Speak, too!

If charnel-houses and our graves must send   70
Those that we bury, back, our monuments
Shall be the maws of kites.   *Exit Ghost*

LADY   What, quite unmanned in folly?

MACBETH

If I stand here, I saw him.

LADY   Fie, for shame!

MACBETH

Blood hath been shed ere now, i'the olden time,
Ere humane statute purged the gentle weal;
Ay, and since too, murders have been performed
Too terrible for the ear. The times has been
That, when the brains were out, the man would die,
And there an end. But now they rise again
With twenty mortal murders on their crowns,   80
And push us from our stools. This is more strange
Than such a murder is.

LADY   My worthy lord,
Your noble friends do lack you.

MACBETH   I do forget.
Do not muse at me, my most worthy friends:
I have a strange infirmity, which is nothing
To those that know me. Come, love and health to all!
Then I'll sit down. Give me some wine; fill full!
     Enter Ghost
I drink to the general joy o'the whole table,
And to our dear friend Banquo, whom we miss.
Would he were here! To all – and him – we thirst,   90
And all to all.

LORDS   Our duties and the pledge!

MACBETH (*sees the Ghost*)

Avaunt, and quit my sight! Let the earth hide thee!
Thy bones are marrowless, thy blood is cold.
Thou hast no speculation in those eyes

Which thou dost glare with.

LADY   Think of this, good peers,
But as a thing of custom; 'tis no other;
Only it spoils the pleasure of the time.

MACBETH
What man dare, I dare.
Approach thou like the rugged Russian bear,
100   The armed rhinoceros, or the Hyrcan tiger,
Take any shape but that, and my firm nerves
Shall never tremble. Or be alive again,
And dare me to the desert with thy sword:
If trembling I inhabit then, protest me
The baby of a girl. Hence, horrible shadow!
Unreal mockery, hence!   *Exit Ghost*
                    Why, so; being gone,
I am a man again. – Pray you sit still.

LADY
You have displaced the mirth, broke the good meeting
With most admired disorder.

MACBETH   Can such things be,
110   And overcome us like a summer's cloud,
Without our special wonder? You make me strange
Even to the disposition that I owe
When now I think you can behold such sights
And keep the natural ruby of your cheeks,
When mine is blanched with fear.

ROSS   What sights, my lord?

LADY
I pray you speak not; he grows worse and worse.
Question enrages him. At once, good night.
Stand not upon the order of your going;
But go at once.

LENNOX   Good night; and better health
120   Attend his majesty!

LADY   A kind good-night to all! *Exeunt Lords*

MACBETH

It will have blood, they say; blood will have blood.
Stones have been known to move and trees to speak;
Augurs and understood relations have
By maggot-pies, and choughs, and rooks brought forth
The secret'st man of blood. What is the night?

LADY

Almost at odds with morning, which is which.

MACBETH

How sayst thou, that Macduff denies his person
At our great bidding?

LADY   Did you send to him, sir?

MACBETH

I hear it by the way. But I will send.
There's not a one of them, but in his house   130
I keep a servant fee'd. I will tomorrow –
And betimes I will – to the Weird Sisters.
More shall they speak; for now I am bent to know
By the worst means the worst. For mine own good
All causes shall give way. I am in blood
Stepped in so far, that, should I wade no more,
Returning were as tedious as go o'er.
Strange things I have in head, that will to hand;
Which must be acted ere they may be scanned.

LADY

You lack the season of all natures, sleep.   140

MACBETH

Come, we'll to sleep. My strange and self-abuse
Is the initiate fear that wants hard use.
We are yet but young in deed.   *Exeunt*

III.5   *Thunder. Enter the three Witches, meeting Hecat*

FIRST WITCH

    Why, how now, Hecat? You look angerly.

HECAT

        Have I not reason, beldams, as you are
        Saucy and over-bold? How did you dare
        To trade and traffic with Macbeth
        In riddles and affairs of death,
        And I, the mistress of your charms,
        The close contriver of all harms,
        Was never called to bear my part,
        Or show the glory of our art?
10   And, which is worse, all you have done
        Hath been but for a wayward son,
        Spiteful and wrathful, who, as others do,
        Loves for his own ends, not for you.
        But make amends now: get you gone,
        And at the pit of Acheron
        Meet me i'the morning. Thither he
        Will come, to know his destiny.
        Your vessels and your spells provide,
        Your charms and everything beside.
20   I am for the air; this night I'll spend
        Unto a dismal and a fatal end.
        Great business must be wrought ere noon
        Upon the corner of the moon:
        There, hangs a vaporous drop profound;
        I'll catch it ere it come to ground;
        And that distilled by magic sleights
        Shall raise such artificial sprites
        As by the strength of their illusion
        Shall draw him on to his confusion.
30   He shall spurn fate, scorn death, and bear
        His hopes 'bove wisdom, grace, and fear.

And you all know security
Is mortals' chiefest enemy.
> *Music and a song*
Hark! I am called. My little spirit, see,
Sits in a foggy cloud and stays for me.
> *Sing within: 'Come away, come away,' etc.*

FIRST WITCH

Come, let's make haste; she'll soon be back again.

> *Exeunt*

> *Enter Lennox and another Lord*   III.6

LENNOX

My former speeches have but hit your thoughts,
Which can interpret further. Only I say
Things have been strangely borne. The gracious Duncan
Was pitied of Macbeth: marry, he was dead!
And the right valiant Banquo walked too late;
Whom you may say, if 't please you, Fleance killed,
For Fleance fled. Men must not walk too late.
Who cannot want the thought how monstrous
It was for Malcolm and for Donalbain
To kill their gracious father? Damnèd fact,   10
How it did grieve Macbeth! Did he not straight –
In pious rage – the two delinquents tear,
That were the slaves of drink, and thralls of sleep?
Was not that nobly done? Ay, and wisely too;
For 'twould have angered any heart alive
To hear the men deny 't. So that I say
He has borne all things well; and I do think
That had he Duncan's sons under his key –
As, an 't please heaven, he shall not – they should find
What 'twere to kill a father – so should Fleance.   20
But, peace! For from broad words, and 'cause he failed

His presence at the tyrant's feast, I hear
Macduff lives in disgrace. Sir, can you tell
Where he bestows himself?

LORD   The son of Duncan,
From whom this tyrant holds the due of birth,
Lives in the English court, and is received
Of the most pious Edward with such grace
That the malevolence of fortune nothing
Takes from his high respect. Thither Macduff
Is gone to pray the holy king, upon his aid,
To wake Northumberland and warlike Seyward,
That by the help of these – with Him above
To ratify the work – we may again
Give to our tables meat, sleep to our nights,
Free from our feasts and banquets bloody knives,
Do faithful homage and receive free honours –
All which we pine for now. And this report
Hath so exasperate the King that he
Prepares for some attempt of war.

LENNOX   Sent he to Macduff?

LORD
He did. And with an absolute 'Sir, not I!'
The cloudy messenger turns me his back
And hums, as who should say 'You'll rue the time
That clogs me with this answer.'

LENNOX   And that well might
Advise him to a caution to hold what distance
His wisdom can provide. Some holy angel
Fly to the court of England and unfold
His message ere he come, that a swift blessing
May soon return to this our suffering country,
Under a hand accursed!

LORD   I'll send my prayers with him.

                                                    Exeunt

*

Thunder. Enter the three Witches   IV.I

FIRST WITCH
> Thrice the brinded cat hath mewed.

SECOND WITCH
> Thrice, and once the hedge-pig whined.

THIRD WITCH
> Harpier cries! 'Tis time, 'tis time!

FIRST WITCH
> Round about the cauldron go;
> In the poisoned entrails throw:
> Toad that under cold stone
> Days and nights has thirty-one.
> Sweltered venom, sleeping got,
> Boil thou first i'the charmèd pot.

ALL
> Double, double, toil and trouble;   10
> Fire burn, and cauldron bubble.

SECOND WITCH
> Fillet of a fenny snake
> In the cauldron boil and bake;
> Eye of newt, and toe of frog,
> Wool of bat, and tongue of dog,
> Adder's fork, and blind-worm's sting,
> Lizard's leg and howlet's wing,
> For a charm of powerful trouble,
> Like a hell-broth, boil and bubble.

ALL
> Double, double, toil and trouble;   20
> Fire burn, and cauldron bubble.

THIRD WITCH
> Scale of dragon, tooth of wolf,

Witch's mummy, maw and gulf
Of the ravined salt sea shark,
Root of hemlock digged i'the dark,
Liver of blaspheming Jew,
Gall of goat, and slips of yew
Slivered in the moon's eclipse,
Nose of Turk, and Tartar's lips,
30   Finger of birth-strangled babe,
Ditch-delivered by a drab,
Make the gruel thick and slab.
Add thereto a tiger's chaudron
For the ingredience of our cauldron.

ALL

Double, double, toil and trouble;
Fire burn, and cauldron bubble.

SECOND WITCH

Cool it with a baboon's blood;
Then the charm is firm and good.
Enter Hecat and the other three Witches

HECAT

O well done! I commend your pains;
40   And everyone shall share i'the gains.
And now about the cauldron sing
Like elves and fairies in a ring,
Enchanting all that you put in.
Music and a song: 'Black spirits' etc.
            Exeunt Hecat and the other three Witches

SECOND WITCH

By the pricking of my thumbs,
Something wicked this way comes.
Open, locks, whoever knocks!
Enter Macbeth

MACBETH

How now, you secret, black, and midnight hags!

What is't you do?

ALL   A deed without a name.

MACBETH

I conjure you, by that which you profess,
Howe'er you come to know it, answer me —   50
Though you untie the winds and let them fight
Against the churches; though the yesty waves
Confound and swallow navigation up;
Though bladed corn be lodged and trees blown down;
Though castles topple on their warders' heads;
Though palaces and pyramids do slope
Their heads to their foundations; though the treasure
Of nature's germens tumble all together
Even till destruction sicken — answer me
To what I ask you.

FIRST WITCH   Speak.

SECOND WITCH   Demand.

THIRD WITCH   We'll answer.   60

FIRST WITCH

Say if thou'dst rather hear it from our mouths
Or from our masters.

MACBETH   Call 'em. Let me see 'em.

FIRST WITCH

                Pour in sow's blood that hath eaten
                Her nine farrow; grease that's sweaten
                From the murderer's gibbet, throw
                Into the flame.

ALL   Come high or low,
                Thyself and office deftly show.

Thunder. First Apparition, an Armed Head

MACBETH

Tell me, thou unknown power —

FIRST WITCH   He knows thy thought.
Hear his speech, but say thou naught.

FIRST APPARITION

70   Macbeth, Macbeth, Macbeth, beware Macduff!
Beware the Thane of Fife! Dismiss me. Enough.

He descends

MACBETH

Whate'er thou art, for thy good caution, thanks;
Thou hast harped my fear aright. But one word more –

FIRST WITCH

He will not be commanded. Here's another
More potent than the first.

Thunder. Second Apparition, a Bloody Child

SECOND APPARITION

Macbeth, Macbeth, Macbeth!

MACBETH

Had I three ears, I'd hear thee.

SECOND APPARITION

Be bloody, bold, and resolute; laugh to scorn
The power of man; for none of woman born

80   Shall harm Macbeth.   *He descends*

MACBETH

Then live Macduff; what need I fear of thee?
But yet I'll make assurance double sure,
And take a bond of fate. Thou shalt not live;
That I may tell pale-hearted fear it lies,
And sleep in spite of thunder.

Thunder. Third Apparition, a Child Crowned, with a tree in his hand

                         What is this
That rises like the issue of a king,
And wears upon his baby brow the round
And top of sovereignty?

ALL   Listen, but speak not to't.

THIRD APPARITION

Be lion-mettled, proud, and take no care

Who chafes, who frets, or where conspirers are;   90
Macbeth shall never vanquished be, until
Great Birnan Wood to high Dunsinane Hill
Shall come against him.   *He descends*
MACBETH   That will never be.
Who can impress the forest, bid the tree
Unfix his earth-bound root? Sweet bodements! Good!
Rebellious dead rise never till the wood
Of Birnan rise, and our high-placed Macbeth
Shall live the lease of nature, pay his breath
To time and mortal custom. Yet my heart
Throbs to know one thing: tell me, if your art   100
Can tell so much, shall Banquo's issue ever
Reign in this kingdom?
ALL   Seek to know no more.
MACBETH
I will be satisfied! Deny me this
And an eternal curse fall on you! Let me know.
Why sinks that cauldron?
    Hautboys
                                And what noise is this?
FIRST WITCH
Show!
SECOND WITCH
Show!
THIRD WITCH
Show!
ALL
        Show his eyes and grieve his heart;
        Come like shadows, so depart.   110
    *A show of eight kings, and Banquo; the last king
    with a glass in his hand*
MACBETH
Thou art too like the spirit of Banquo. Down!

Thy crown does sear mine eye-balls. And thy hair,
Thou other gold-bound brow, is like the first.
A third is like the former. – Filthy hags,
Why do you show me this? – A fourth? Start, eyes!
What, will the line stretch out to the crack of doom?
Another yet? A seventh? I'll see no more!
And yet the eighth appears, who bears a glass
Which shows me many more. And some I see
120   That two-fold balls and treble sceptres carry.
Horrible sight! Now I see 'tis true,
For the blood-boltered Banquo smiles upon me,
And points at them for his. What! Is this so?

FIRST WITCH

      Ay, sir, all this is so. But why
      Stands Macbeth thus amazedly?
      Come, sisters, cheer we up his sprites
      And show the best of our delights.
      I'll charm the air to give a sound,
      While you perform your antic round,
130   That this great king may kindly say
      Our duties did his welcome pay.

Music. The Witches dance; and vanish

MACBETH

Where are they? Gone! Let this pernicious hour
Stand aye accursèd in the calendar.
Come in, without there.

Enter Lennox

LENNOX   What's your grace's will?

MACBETH

Saw you the Weird Sisters?

LENNOX   No, my lord.

MACBETH

Came they not by you?

LENNOX   No, indeed, my lord.

MACBETH

  Infected be the air whereon they ride,
  And damned all those that trust them. I did hear
  The galloping of horse. Who was't came by?

LENNOX

  'Tis two or three, my lord, that bring you word   140
  Macduff is fled to England.

MACBETH   Fled to England!

LENNOX

  Ay, my good lord.

MACBETH

  Time, thou anticipat'st my dread exploits.
  The flighty purpose never is o'ertook
  Unless the deed go with it. From this moment
  The very firstlings of my heart shall be
  The firstlings of my hand. And even now,
  To crown my thoughts with acts, be it thought and done:
  The castle of Macduff I will surprise,
  Seize upon Fife, give to the edge o'the sword   150
  His wife, his babes, and all unfortunate souls
  That trace him in his line. No boasting, like a fool;
  This deed I'll do before this purpose cool.
  But no more sights! – Where are these gentlemen?
  Come, bring me where they are.   *Exeunt*

    Enter Macduff's Wife, her Son, and Ross   IV.2

WIFE

  What had he done to make him fly the land?

ROSS

  You must have patience, madam.

WIFE   He had none.

  His flight was madness; when our actions do not,

    Our fears do make us traitors.

ROSS   You know not
    Whether it was his wisdom or his fear.

WIFE

    Wisdom! To leave his wife, to leave his babes,
    His mansion and his titles, in a place
    From whence himself does fly? He loves us not.
    He wants the natural touch; for the poor wren,
10   The most diminutive of birds, will fight,
    Her young ones in her nest, against the owl.
    All is the fear and nothing is the love,
    As little is the wisdom, where the flight
    So runs against all reason.

ROSS   My dearest cuz,
    I pray you school yourself. But, for your husband,
    He is noble, wise, judicious, and best knows
    The fits o'the season. I dare not speak much further,
    But cruel are the times when we are traitors
    And do not know, ourselves; when we hold rumour
20   From what we fear, yet know not what we fear,
    But float upon a wild and violent sea,
    Each way and move. I take my leave of you;
    Shall not be long but I'll be here again.
    Things at the worst will cease or else climb upward
    To what they were before. – My pretty cousin,
    Blessing upon you!

WIFE

    Fathered he is, and yet he's fatherless.

ROSS

    I am so much a fool, should I stay longer
    It would be my disgrace and your discomfort.
30   I take my leave at once.   *Exit*

WIFE

    Sirrah, your father's dead.

And what will you do now? How will you live?

SON

As birds do, mother.

WIFE   What, with worms and flies?

SON

With what I get, I mean; and so do they.

WIFE

Poor bird, thou'dst never fear
The net nor lime, the pitfall nor the gin!

SON

Why should I, mother? Poor birds they are not set for.
My father is not dead, for all your saying.

WIFE

Yes, he is dead. How wilt thou do for a father?

SON Nay, how will you do for a husband?   40

WIFE Why, I can buy me twenty at any market.

SON Then you'll buy 'em to sell again.

WIFE

Thou speak'st with all thy wit;
And yet, i'faith, with wit enough for thee.

SON Was my father a traitor, mother?

WIFE Ay, that he was.

SON What is a traitor?

WIFE Why, one that swears and lies.

SON And be all traitors that do so?

WIFE

Every one that does so is a traitor,   50
And must be hanged.

SON

And must they all be hanged that swear and lie?

WIFE Every one.

SON Who must hang them?

WIFE Why, the honest men.

SON Then the liars and swearers are fools; for there are

liars and swearers enow to beat the honest men and hang
up them.

WIFE Now God help thee, poor monkey! But how wilt
thou do for a father?

SON If he were dead, you'd weep for him; if you would
not, it were a good sign that I should quickly have a new
father.

WIFE Poor prattler, how thou talk'st!

Enter a Messenger

MESSENGER
Bless you, fair dame! I am not to you known,
Though in your state of honour I am perfect.
I doubt some danger does approach you nearly.
If you will take a homely man's advice,
Be not found here. Hence with your little ones!
To fright you thus methinks I am too savage;
To do worse to you were fell cruelty,
Which is too nigh your person. Heaven preserve you!
I dare abide no longer.   *Exit*

WIFE   Whither should I fly?
I have done no harm. But I remember now
I am in this earthly world, where to do harm
Is often laudable, to do good sometime
Accounted dangerous folly. Why then, alas,
Do I put up that womanly defence
To say I have done no harm?

Enter Murderers
                                      What are these faces?

MURDERER
Where is your husband?

WIFE
I hope in no place so unsanctified
Where such as thou mayst find him.

MURDERER   He's a traitor.

SON

   Thou liest, thou shag-haired villain!

MURDERER   What, you egg,

   Young fry of treachery!

    He stabs him

SON   He has killed me, mother!

   Run away, I pray you.

             Son dies. Exit Wife crying 'Murder'

   Enter Malcolm and Macduff   IV.3

MALCOLM

   Let us seek out some desolate shade, and there

   Weep our sad bosoms empty.

MACDUFF   Let us rather

   Hold fast the mortal sword; and like good men

   Bestride our down-fallen birthdom. Each new morn

   New widows howl, new orphans cry, new sorrows

   Strike heaven on the face, that it resounds

   As if it felt with Scotland, and yelled out

   Like syllable of dolour.

MALCOLM   What I believe, I'll wail;

   What know, believe; and what I can redress,

   As I shall find the time to friend, I will.

   What you have spoke, it may be so perchance.   10

   This tyrant, whose sole name blisters our tongues,

   Was once thought honest; you have loved him well;

   He hath not touched you yet. I am young; but something

   You may deserve of him, through me; and wisdom

   To offer up a weak poor innocent lamb

   T'appease an angry god.

MACDUFF

   I am not treacherous.

MALCOLM   But Macbeth is.

A good and virtuous nature may recoil
20   In an imperial charge. But I shall crave your pardon:
That which you are my thoughts cannot transpose;
Angels are bright still though the brightest fell.
Though all things foul would wear the brows of grace,
Yet grace must still look so.

MACDUFF   I have lost my hopes.

MALCOLM

Perchance even there where I did find my doubts.
Why in that rawness left you wife and child,
Those precious motives, those strong knots of love,
Without leave-taking? I pray you,
Let not my jealousies be your dishonours
30   But mine own safeties. You may be rightly just,
Whatever I shall think.

MACDUFF   Bleed, bleed, poor country!
Great tyranny, lay thou thy basis sure,
For goodness dare not check thee; wear thou thy wrongs,
The title is affeered. Fare thee well, lord!
I would not be the villain that thou think'st
For the whole space that's in the tyrant's grasp,
And the rich East to boot.

MALCOLM   Be not offended;
I speak not as in absolute fear of you.
I think our country sinks beneath the yoke,
40   It weeps, it bleeds, and each new day a gash
Is added to her wounds. I think withal
There would be hands uplifted in my right;
And here from gracious England have I offer
Of goodly thousands. But for all this,
When I shall tread upon the tyrant's head
Or wear it on my sword, yet my poor country
Shall have more vices than it had before,
More suffer, and more sundry ways, than ever,

By him that shall succeed.
MACDUFF   What should he be?
MALCOLM
It is myself I mean; in whom I know   50
All the particulars of vice so grafted
That, when they shall be opened, black Macbeth
Will seem as pure as snow and the poor state
Esteem him as a lamb, being compared
With my confineless harms.
MACDUFF   Not in the legions
Of horrid hell can come a devil more damned
In evils to top Macbeth.
MALCOLM   I grant him bloody,
Luxurious, avaricious, false, deceitful,
Sudden, malicious, smacking of every sin
That has a name. But there's no bottom, none,   60
In my voluptuousness. Your wives, your daughters,
Your matrons, and your maids, could not fill up
The cistern of my lust; and my desire
All continent impediments would o'erbear
That did oppose my will. Better Macbeth
Than such a one to reign.
MACDUFF   Boundless intemperance
In nature is a tyranny. It hath been
The untimely emptying of the happy throne,
And fall of many kings. But fear not yet
To take upon you what is yours. You may   70
Convey your pleasures in a spacious plenty
And yet seem cold; the time you may so hoodwink.
We have willing dames enough. There cannot be
That vulture in you to devour so many
As will to greatness dedicate themselves,
Finding it so inclined.
MALCOLM   With this there grows

In my most ill-composed affection such
A staunchless avarice that, were I king,
I should cut off the nobles for their lands,
80   Desire his jewels and this other's house,
And my more-having would be as a sauce
To make me hunger more, that I should forge
Quarrels unjust against the good and loyal,
Destroying them for wealth.

MACDUFF   This avarice
Sticks deeper, grows with more pernicious root
Than summer-seeming lust; and it hath been
The sword of our slain kings. Yet do not fear:
Scotland hath foisons to fill up your will
Of your mere own. All these are portable,
90   With other graces weighed.

MALCOLM   But I have none.
The king-becoming graces,
As justice, verity, temperance, stableness,
Bounty, perseverance, mercy, lowliness,
Devotion, patience, courage, fortitude,
I have no relish of them, but abound
In the division of each several crime,
Acting it many ways. Nay, had I power, I should
Pour the sweet milk of concord into hell,
Uproar the universal peace, confound
100 All unity on earth.

MACDUFF   O Scotland, Scotland!

MALCOLM
If such a one be fit to govern, speak.
I am as I have spoken.

MACDUFF   Fit to govern!
No, not to live! O nation miserable,
With an untitled tyrant, bloody-sceptred,
When shalt thou see thy wholesome days again,

Since that the truest issue of thy throne
By his own interdiction stands accused
And does blaspheme his breed? Thy royal father
Was a most sainted king; the queen that bore thee,
Oftener upon her knees than on her feet,   110
Died every day she lived. Fare thee well!
These evils thou repeat'st upon thyself
Hath banished me from Scotland. O my breast,
Thy hope ends here!

MALCOLM   Macduff, this noble passion,
Child of integrity, hath from my soul
Wiped the black scruples, reconciled my thoughts
To thy good truth and honour. Devilish Macbeth
By many of these trains hath sought to win me
Into his power, and modest wisdom plucks me
From over-credulous haste. But God above   120
Deal between thee and me; for even now
I put myself to thy direction, and
Unspeak mine own detraction, here abjure
The taints and blames I laid upon myself
For strangers to my nature. I am yet
Unknown to woman, never was forsworn,
Scarcely have coveted what was mine own,
At no time broke my faith, would not betray
The devil to his fellow, and delight
No less in truth than life. My first false speaking   130
Was this upon myself. What I am truly
Is thine and my poor country's to command;
Whither indeed, before thy here-approach,
Old Seyward with ten thousand warlike men,
Already at a point, was setting forth.
Now we'll together; and the chance of goodness
Be like our warranted quarrel! Why are you silent?

MACDUFF

    Such welcome and unwelcome things at once
    'Tis hard to reconcile.

      Enter a Doctor

MALCOLM   Well, more anon. –

140   Comes the King forth, I pray you?

DOCTOR

    Ay, sir. There are a crew of wretched souls
    That stay his cure. Their malady convinces
    The great assay of art; but at his touch,
    Such sanctity hath heaven given his hand,
    They presently amend.

MALCOLM   I thank you, doctor.

                                      Exit Doctor

MACDUFF

    What's the disease he means?

MALCOLM   'Tis called the Evil –

    A most miraculous work in this good king,
    Which often since my here-remain in England
    I have seen him do. How he solicits heaven

150   Himself best knows: but strangely visited people,
    All swollen and ulcerous, pitiful to the eye,
    The mere despair of surgery, he cures,
    Hanging a golden stamp about their necks
    Put on with holy prayers; and 'tis spoken,
    To the succeeding royalty he leaves
    The healing benediction. With this strange virtue
    He hath a heavenly gift of prophecy,
    And sundry blessings hang about his throne
    That speak him full of grace.

      Enter Ross

MACDUFF   See who comes here.

MALCOLM

160   My countryman; but yet I know him not.

MACDUFF

My ever gentle cousin, welcome hither.

MALCOLM

I know him now. Good God betimes remove
The means that makes us strangers!

ROSS   Sir, amen.

MACDUFF

Stands Scotland where it did?

ROSS   Alas, poor country,
Almost afraid to know itself! It cannot
Be called our mother, but our grave; where nothing
But who knows nothing is once seen to smile;
Where sighs and groans and shrieks that rent the air
Are made, not marked; where violent sorrow seems
A modern ecstasy. The dead man's knell   170
Is there scarce asked for who, and good men's lives
Expire before the flowers in their caps,
Dying or ere they sicken.

MACDUFF   O relation
Too nice and yet too true.

MALCOLM   What's the newest grief?

ROSS

That of an hour's age doth hiss the speaker;
Each minute teems a new one.

MACDUFF   How does my wife?

ROSS

Why, well.

MACDUFF

          And all my children?

ROSS   Well too.

MACDUFF

The tyrant has not battered at their peace?

ROSS

No. They were well at peace when I did leave 'em.

MACDUFF

180   Be not a niggard of your speech. How goes't?

ROSS

When I came hither to transport the tidings
Which I have heavily borne, there ran a rumour
Of many worthy fellows that were out,
Which was to my belief witnessed the rather
For that I saw the tyrant's power afoot.
Now is the time of help. (*To Malcolm*) Your eye in
    Scotland
Would create soldiers, make our women fight
To doff their dire distresses.

MALCOLM   Be't their comfort
We are coming thither. Gracious England hath

190   Lent us good Seyward and ten thousand men –
An older and a better soldier none
That Christendom gives out.

ROSS   Would I could answer
This comfort with the like. But I have words
That would be howled out in the desert air,
Where hearing should not latch them.

MACDUFF   What concern they?
The general cause, or is it a fee-grief
Due to some single breast?

ROSS   No mind that's honest
But in it shares some woe, though the main part
Pertains to you alone.

MACDUFF   If it be mine,

200   Keep it not from me; quickly let me have it.

ROSS

Let not your ears despise my tongue for ever,
Which shall possess them with the heaviest sound
That ever yet they heard.

MACDUFF   Humh! I guess at it.

ROSS

    Your castle is surprised, your wife and babes
    Savagely slaughtered. To relate the manner
    Were on the quarry of these murdered deer
    To add the death of you.

MALCOLM   Merciful heaven!

    What, man! Ne'er pull your hat upon your brows.
    Give sorrow words: the grief that does not speak
    Whispers the o'erfraught heart and bids it break.   210

MACDUFF

    My children too?

ROSS   Wife, children, servants, all

    That could be found.

MACDUFF   And I must be from thence!

    My wife killed too?

ROSS   I have said.

MALCOLM   Be comforted.

    Let's make us medicines of our great revenge
    To cure this deadly grief.

MACDUFF   He has no children.

    All my pretty ones? Did you say all?
    O hell-kite! All? What, all my pretty chickens
    And their dam, at one fell swoop?

MALCOLM

    Dispute it like a man.

MACDUFF   I shall do so;

    But I must also feel it as a man.   220
    I cannot but remember such things were
    That were most precious to me. Did heaven look on
    And would not take their part? Sinful Macduff!
    They were all struck for thee. Naught that I am,
    Not for their own demerits, but for mine,
    Fell slaughter on their souls. Heaven rest them now!

MALCOLM

    Be this the whetstone of your sword; let grief
    Convert to anger; blunt not the heart, enrage it.

MACDUFF

    O, I could play the woman with mine eyes
230   And braggart with my tongue! But, gentle heavens,
    Cut short all intermission. Front to front
    Bring thou this fiend of Scotland and myself.
    Within my sword's length set him; if he scape,
    Heaven forgive him too.

MALCOLM   This tune goes manly.

    Come, go we to the King; our power is ready;
    Our lack is nothing but our leave. Macbeth
    Is ripe for shaking, and the powers above
    Put on their instruments. Receive what cheer you may:
    The night is long that never finds the day.   *Exeunt*

*

V.I   *Enter a Doctor of Physic and a Waiting-Gentlewoman*

    DOCTOR I have two nights watched with you, but can
    perceive no truth in your report. When was it she last
    walked?

    GENTLEWOMAN Since his majesty went into the field I
    have seen her rise from her bed, throw her nightgown
    upon her, unlock her closet, take forth paper, fold it,
    write upon't, read it, afterwards seal it, and again return
    to bed; yet all this while in a most fast sleep.

    DOCTOR A great perturbation in nature, to receive at once
10   the benefit of sleep and do the effects of watching. In
    this slumbery agitation, besides her walking and other
    actual performances, what, at any time, have you heard
    her say?

GENTLEWOMAN That, sir, which I will not report after
her.

DOCTOR You may to me; and 'tis most meet you should.

GENTLEWOMAN Neither to you nor anyone, having no
witness to confirm my speech.

Enter Lady Macbeth with a taper

Lo you! Here she comes. This is her very guise; and,
upon my life, fast asleep. Observe her; stand close.   20

DOCTOR How came she by that light?

GENTLEWOMAN Why, it stood by her. She has light by
her continually; 'tis her command.

DOCTOR You see her eyes are open.

GENTLEWOMAN Ay, but their sense are shut.

DOCTOR What is it she does now? Look how she rubs her
hands.

GENTLEWOMAN It is an accustomed action with her to
seem thus washing her hands. I have known her continue in this a quarter of an hour.

LADY Yet here's a spot.   30

DOCTOR Hark! She speaks. I will set down what comes
from her, to satisfy my remembrance the more strongly.

LADY Out, damned spot! Out, I say! – One: two: why
then, 'tis time to do't. – Hell is murky! – Fie, my lord,
fie! A soldier and afeard? – What need we fear who
knows it, when none can call our power to accompt? –
Yet who would have thought the old man to have had so
much blood in him?

DOCTOR Do you mark that?   40

LADY The Thane of Fife had a wife; where is she now? –
What, will these hands ne'er be clean? – No more o'that,
my lord, no more o'that. You mar all with this starting.

DOCTOR Go to, go to: you have known what you should
not.

GENTLEWOMAN She has spoke what she should not, I am

sure of that. Heaven knows what she has known.

LADY Here's the smell of the blood still. All the perfumes of Arabia will not sweeten this little hand. Oh! Oh! Oh!

50 DOCTOR What a sigh is there! The heart is sorely charged.

GENTLEWOMAN I would not have such a heart in my bosom for the dignity of the whole body.

DOCTOR Well, well, well.

GENTLEWOMAN Pray God it be, sir.

DOCTOR This disease is beyond my practice; yet I have known those which have walked in their sleep who have died holily in their beds.

LADY Wash your hands; put on your nightgown; look not so pale. I tell you yet again, Banquo's buried; he cannot

60 come out on's grave.

DOCTOR Even so?

LADY To bed, to bed! There's knocking at the gate. Come, come, come, come, give me your hand. What's done cannot be undone. To bed, to bed, to bed.

                                                Exit

DOCTOR Will she go now to bed?

GENTLEWOMAN Directly.

DOCTOR

Foul whisperings are abroad, unnatural deeds
Do breed unnatural troubles; infected minds
To their deaf pillows will discharge their secrets.

70 More needs she the divine than the physician.
God, God forgive us all! Look after her,
Remove from her the means of all annoyance
And still keep eyes upon her. So, good night.
My mind she has mated, and amazed my sight.
I think, but dare not speak.

GENTLEWOMAN   Good night, good doctor.

                                                Exeunt

Drum and colours. Enter Menteth, Cathness, Angus,   **V.2**
Lennox, Soldiers

MENTETH
   The English power is near, led on by Malcolm,
   His uncle Seyward and the good Macduff.
   Revenges burn in them; for their dear causes
   Would to the bleeding and the grim alarm
   Excite the mortified man.

ANGUS   Near Birnan Wood
   Shall we well meet them; that way are they coming.

CATHNESS
   Who knows if Donalbain be with his brother?

LENNOX
   For certain, sir, he is not. I have a file
   Of all the gentry: there is Seyward's son
   And many unrough youths that even now   10
   Protest their first of manhood.

MENTETH   What does the tyrant?

CATHNESS
   Great Dunsinane he strongly fortifies.
   Some say he's mad. Others, that lesser hate him,
   Do call it valiant fury; but for certain
   He cannot buckle his distempered cause
   Within the belt of rule.

ANGUS   Now does he feel
   His secret murders sticking on his hands;
   Now minutely revolts upbraid his faith-breach.
   Those he commands move only in command,
   Nothing in love. Now does he feel his title   20
   Hang loose about him like a giant's robe
   Upon a dwarfish thief.

MENTETH   Who then shall blame
   His pestered senses to recoil and start,
   When all that is within him does condemn

Itself for being there?

CATHNESS   Well, march we on
To give obedience where 'tis truly owed.
Meet we the medicine of the sickly weal,
And with him pour we in our country's purge
Each drop of us.

LENNOX   Or so much as it needs
30 To dew the sovereign flower and drown the weeds.
Make we our march towards Birnan. *Exeunt, marching*

V.3   *Enter Macbeth, Doctor, and Attendants*

MACBETH
Bring me no more reports; let them fly all.
Till Birnan Wood remove to Dunsinane
I cannot taint with fear. What's the boy Malcolm?
Was he not born of woman? The spirits that know
All mortal consequences have pronounced me thus:
'Fear not, Macbeth; no man that's born of woman
Shall e'er have power upon thee.' Then fly, false thanes,
And mingle with the English epicures.
The mind I sway by and the heart I bear
10 Shall never sag with doubt nor shake with fear.
     Enter Servant
The devil damn thee black, thou cream-faced loon!
Where got'st thou that goose look?

SERVANT
There is ten thousand –

MACBETH   Geese, villain?

SERVANT   Soldiers, sir.

MACBETH
Go prick thy face and over-red thy fear,
Thou lily-livered boy. What soldiers, patch?
Death of thy soul! Those linen cheeks of thine

Are counsellors to fear. What soldiers, whey-face?

SERVANT

The English force, so please you.

MACBETH

Take thy face hence.   *Exit Servant*
                    Seyton! – I am sick at heart
When I behold – Seyton, I say! – This push   20
Will chair me ever or dis-seat me now.
I have lived long enough: my way of life
Is fallen into the sere, the yellow leaf;
And that which should accompany old age,
As honour, love, obedience, troops of friends,
I must not look to have; but, in their stead,
Curses, not loud, but deep, mouth-honour, breath
Which the poor heart would fain deny and dare not.
Seyton!

    Enter Seyton

SEYTON

What's your gracious pleasure?

MACBETH   What news more?   30

SEYTON

All is confirmed, my lord, which was reported.

MACBETH

I'll fight till from my bones my flesh be hacked.
Give me my armour.

SEYTON   'Tis not needed yet.

MACBETH

I'll put it on.
Send out more horses, skirr the country round,
Hang those that talk of fear. – Give me mine armour. –
How does your patient, doctor?

DOCTOR   Not so sick, my lord,
As she is troubled with thick-coming fancies
That keep her from her rest.

MACBETH   Cure her of that.

40   Canst thou not minister to a mind diseased,
      Pluck from the memory a rooted sorrow,
      Raze out the written troubles of the brain,
      And with some sweet oblivious antidote
      Cleanse the stuffed bosom of that perilous stuff
      Which weighs upon the heart?

DOCTOR   Therein the patient
      Must minister to himself.

MACBETH
      Throw physic to the dogs! I'll none of it. –
      Come, put mine armour on, give me my staff.
      Seyton, send out. – Doctor, the thanes fly from me. –
50   Come, sir, dispatch. – If thou couldst, doctor, cast
      The water of my land, find her disease
      And purge it to a sound and pristine health,
      I would applaud thee to the very echo
      That should applaud again. – Pull't off, I say. –
      What rhubarb, senna, or what purgative drug
      Would scour these English hence? Hear'st thou of them?

DOCTOR
      Ay, my good lord; your royal preparation
      Makes us hear something.

MACBETH   – Bring it after me.
      I will not be afraid of death and bane
60   Till Birnan forest come to Dunsinane.   *Exit*

DOCTOR
      Were I from Dunsinane away and clear,
      Profit again should hardly draw me here.   *Exit*

Drum and colours. Enter Malcolm, Seyward, Mac-   V.4
duff, Seyward's Son, Menteth, Cathness, Angus,
and Soldiers marching

MALCOLM
Cousins, I hope the days are near at hand
That chambers will be safe.

MENTETH   We doubt it nothing.

SEYWARD
What wood is this before us?

MENTETH   The wood of Birnan.

MALCOLM
Let every soldier hew him down a bough
And bear't before him; thereby shall we shadow
The numbers of our host and make discovery
Err in report of us.

SOLDIERS   It shall be done.

SEYWARD
We learn no other but the confident tyrant
Keeps still in Dunsinane and will endure
Our setting down before't.

MALCOLM   'Tis his main hope.   10
For where there is advantage to be given,
Both more and less have given him the revolt,
And none serve with him but constrainèd things
Whose hearts are absent too.

MACDUFF   Let our just censures
Attend the true event, and put we on
Industrious soldiership.

SEYWARD   The time approaches
That will with due decision make us know
What we shall say we have, and what we owe.
Thoughts speculative their unsure hopes relate,
But certain issue strokes must arbitrate;   20
Towards which, advance the war.   *Exeunt, marching*

V.5   *Enter Macbeth, Seyton, and Soldiers, with drum and*
              colours

MACBETH

   Hang out our banners on the outward walls.
   The cry is still, 'They come.' Our castle's strength
   Will laugh a siege to scorn. Here let them lie
   Till famine and the ague eat them up.
   Were they not farced with those that should be ours
   We might have met them dareful, beard to beard,
   And beat them backward home.

   A cry within of women

                             What is that noise?

SEYTON

   It is the cry of women, my good lord.   *Exit*

MACBETH

   I have almost forgot the taste of fears.
10   The time has been my senses would have cooled
   To hear a night-shriek, and my fell of hair
   Would at a dismal treatise rouse and stir
   As life were in't. I have supped full with horrors:
   Direness, familiar to my slaughterous thoughts,
   Cannot once start me.

   Enter Seyton

                      Wherefore was that cry?

SEYTON

   The queen, my lord, is dead.

MACBETH

   She should have died hereafter.
   There would have been a time for such a word –
   Tomorrow, and tomorrow, and tomorrow,
20   Creeps in this petty pace from day to day
   To the last syllable of recorded time;
   And all our yesterdays have lighted fools
   The way to dusty death. Out, out, brief candle!

Life's but a walking shadow, a poor player
That struts and frets his hour upon the stage
And then is heard no more. It is a tale
Told by an idiot, full of sound and fury,
Signifying nothing.

    Enter a Messenger

Thou com'st to use thy tongue: thy story quickly!

MESSENGER

  Gracious my lord,   30
  I should report that which I say I saw,
  But know not how to do't.

MACBETH   Well, say, sir.

MESSENGER

  As I did stand my watch upon the hill
  I looked toward Birnan and anon methought
  The wood began to move.

MACBETH   Liar and slave!

MESSENGER

  Let me endure your wrath if 't be not so.
  Within this three mile may you see it coming.
  I say, a moving grove.

MACBETH   If thou speak'st false,
Upon the next tree shall thou hang alive
Till famine cling thee. If thy speech be sooth,   40
I care not if thou dost for me as much.
I pull in resolution, and begin
To doubt the equivocation of the fiend
That lies like truth. 'Fear not till Birnan Wood
Do come to Dunsinane' – and now a wood
Comes toward Dunsinane. Arm, arm, and out!
If this which he avouches does appear,
There is nor flying hence nor tarrying here.
I 'gin to be aweary of the sun,
And wish the estate o'the world were now undone. –   50

Ring the alarum bell! – Blow wind, come wrack,
At least we'll die with harness on our back.   *Exeunt*

V.6   *Drum and colours. Enter Malcolm, Seyward, Mac-*
         duff, and their army, with boughs

MALCOLM
    Now near enough. Your leavy screens throw down,
    And show like those you are. You, worthy uncle,
    Shall with my cousin, your right noble son,
    Lead our first battle. Worthy Macduff and we
    Shall take upon's what else remains to do,
    According to our order.

SEYWARD   Fare you well.
    Do we but find the tyrant's power tonight,
    Let us be beaten if we cannot fight.

MACDUFF
    Make all our trumpets speak, give them all breath,
10 Those clamorous harbingers of blood and death.
                                             Exeunt

         Alarums continued
         Enter Macbeth

MACBETH
    They have tied me to a stake, I cannot fly,
    But bear-like I must fight the course. What's he
    That was not born of woman? Such a one
    Am I to fear, or none.
         Enter Young Seyward

YOUNG SEYWARD
    What is thy name?

MACBETH   Thou'lt be afraid to hear it.

YOUNG SEYWARD
    No, though thou call'st thyself a hotter name
    Than any is in hell.

MACBETH   My name's Macbeth.

YOUNG SEYWARD

The devil himself could not pronounce a title
More hateful to mine ear.

MACBETH   No, nor more fearful.

YOUNG SEYWARD

Thou liest, abhorrèd tyrant! With my sword   20
I'll prove the lie thou speak'st.

Fight, and Young Seyward slain

MACBETH   Thou wast born of woman.

But swords I smile at, weapons laugh to scorn,
Brandished by man that's of a woman born.   *Exit*

Alarums. Enter Macduff

MACDUFF

That way the noise is. Tyrant, show thy face.
If thou be'st slain, and with no stroke of mine,
My wife and children's ghosts will haunt me still.
I cannot strike at wretched kerns, whose arms
Are hired to bear their staves. Either thou, Macbeth,
Or else my sword with an unbattered edge
I sheathe again undeeded. There thou shouldst be: 30
By this great clatter one of greatest note
Seems bruited. Let me find him, fortune!
And more I beg not.   *Exit*

Alarums. Enter Malcolm and Seyward

SEYWARD

This way, my lord. The castle's gently rendered.
The tyrant's people on both sides do fight;
The noble thanes do bravely in the war;
The day almost itself professes yours,
And little is to do.

MALCOLM   We have met with foes

That strike beside us.

SEYWARD   Enter, sir, the castle.   *Exeunt*

Alarum. Enter Macbeth

MACBETH

40   Why should I play the Roman fool and die
On mine own sword? Whiles I see lives, the gashes
Do better upon them.

    Enter Macduff

MACDUFF   Turn, hellhound, turn!

MACBETH

Of all men else I have avoided thee.
But get thee back; my soul is too much charged
With blood of thine already.

MACDUFF   I have no words;
My voice is in my sword, thou bloodier villain
Than terms can give thee out.

    Fight. Alarum

MACBETH   Thou losest labour.
As easy mayst thou the intrenchant air
With thy keen sword impress, as make me bleed.

50   Let fall thy blade on vulnerable crests,
I bear a charmèd life which must not yield
To one of woman born.

MACDUFF   Despair thy charm,
And let the angel whom thou still hast served
Tell thee Macduff was from his mother's womb
Untimely ripped.

MACBETH

Accursèd be that tongue that tells me so;
For it hath cowed my better part of man;
And be these juggling fiends no more believed
That palter with us in a double sense,

60   That keep the word of promise to our ear
And break it to our hope. I'll not fight with thee.

MACDUFF

Then yield thee, coward;

And live to be the show and gaze o'the time.
We'll have thee, as our rarer monsters are,
Painted upon a pole, and underwrit,
'Here may you see the tyrant.'
MACBETH   I will not yield
To kiss the ground before young Malcolm's feet
And to be baited with the rabble's curse.
Though Birnan Wood be come to Dunsinane
And thou opposed, being of no woman born,   70
Yet I will try the last. Before my body
I throw my warlike shield. Lay on, Macduff;
And damned be him that first cries, 'Hold, enough!'
                                        Exeunt fighting
     Alarums. Enter fighting, and Macbeth slain

                                        Exit Macduff
     Retreat and flourish. Enter with drum and colours
     Malcolm, Seyward, Ross, Thanes, and Soldiers
MALCOLM
I would the friends we miss were safe arrived.
SEYWARD
Some must go off; and yet, by these I see
So great a day as this is cheaply bought.
MALCOLM
Macduff is missing and your noble son.
ROSS
Your son, my lord, has paid a soldier's debt.
He only lived but till he was a man;
The which no sooner had his prowess confirmed   80
In the unshrinking station where he fought
But, like a man, he died.
SEYWARD   Then he is dead?
ROSS
Ay, and brought off the field. Your cause of sorrow
Must not be measured by his worth, for then

It hath no end.
SEYWARD   Had he his hurts before?
ROSS

Ay, on the front.
SEYWARD   Why then, God's soldier be he.
Had I as many sons as I have hairs
I would not wish them to a fairer death.
And so his knell is knolled.
MALCOLM   He's worth more sorrow;
90   And that I'll spend for him.
SEYWARD   He's worth no more:
They say he parted well, and paid his score.
And so God be with him. — Here comes newer comfort.
        Enter Macduff with Macbeth's head

MACDUFF

Hail, King! For so thou art. Behold where stands
The usurper's cursèd head. The time is free.
I see thee compassed with thy kingdom's pearl
That speak my salutation in their minds,
Whose voices I desire aloud with mine. —
Hail, King of Scotland!
ALL   Hail, King of Scotland!
        Flourish

MALCOLM

We shall not spend a large expense of time
100   Before we reckon with your several loves,
And make us even with you. My thanes and kinsmen,
Henceforth be earls, the first that ever Scotland
In such an honour named. What's more to do,
Which would be planted newly with the time,
As calling home our exiled friends abroad
That fled the snares of watchful tyranny,
Producing forth the cruel ministers
Of this dead butcher and his fiend-like queen —

Who, as 'tis thought, by self and violent hands
Took off her life – this, and what needful else   110
That calls upon us, by the grace of Grace
We will perform in measure, time, and place.
So thanks to all at once, and to each one,
Whom we invite to see us crowned at Scone.

Flourish. Exeunt

An Account of the Text

THE NAMES OF THE CHARACTERS

The Folio's names for the characters in *Macbeth* are consistent and do not require emendation to make them intelligible; but editors have regularly changed some of them in the interest of historical accuracy or modern usage. In the Folio (referred to below and in the Commentary as F) Lady Macbeth is regularly referred to as *Lady*, Duncan as *King*, Lady Macduff as *Wife* (*Macduff's Wife* in the entry to IV.2), and these I have preserved as possible indicators of the author's sense of their roles. To modernize names is to give historical specificity to persons and places that have their meaning inside the play and not in atlases and textbooks. 'Banwho' is no doubt the correct phonetic rendering of Banquo (= Banquho) but it would be mere pedantry to print it. Shakespeare's *Hecat* (two syllables) is not the classical Hecate (three syllables); his *Birnan* is not the Birnam that can be found on a map. His *Cathness* and *Menteth* are not the modern Caithness and Menteith, but names he found in Holinshed and fitted (in these forms) into his versification.

The *Other MURDERERS* who appear in the list of characters are those who murder Lady Macduff and her son. These are dramatically distinct from the *Three MURDERERS* with whom Macbeth arranges the murder of Banquo. The *other three Witches* who enter with Hecat at IV.1.38 seem to be different from the *Weird Sisters* found elsewhere.

THE SOURCE OF THE TEXT

Macbeth first appeared in the collected volume of Shakespeare's plays (1623), the so-called first Folio. The text found there has been the subject of much suspicion (like almost everything in that famous volume). The play is shorter than any other tragedy (about 2,100 lines). This does not mean, however, that it has been shortened. The text as we have it is entirely intelligible, orderly and coherent (acts and scenes are regularly marked). This means that there has not been much room for displays of textual ingenuity. W. W. Greg, in *The Shakespeare First Folio* (1955), summarizes the standard assumptions. It is usually supposed that the printers of F set their text from the theatre's prompt book (or a transcript of it). The editor's function is therefore to follow the Folio text except where there are manifest printing errors (not collated below) or where the intention of the passage seems to be contradicted by the F reading. A list of these latter cases is given. The alternative reading printed is that of F, except that long 's' (ʃ) is not used.

THE INTEGRITY OF THE TEXT

The songs and associated dialogue in III.5 and IV.1 (called 'interpolations' in the Commentary (headnote to III.5)) have recently been redescribed as 'contributions' by Thomas Middleton, acting as Shakespeare's collaborator (this has led to even larger claims for Middleton's authorship in *Macbeth*). The Oxford editors and Nicholas Brooke have responded to this claim by putting into the text all the elaborations of F that appear in the manuscript of Middleton's *The Witch* and in Davenant's version of *Macbeth*, with flying ascents and descents, choral interludes and a singing cat (whose Muse is 'mews').

It is clear that these operatic confections are part of the stage history of *Macbeth* (which continued to rely on the charms of 'new songs' to sell new editions up to 1785), and it is equally

clear that Shakespeare's text cannot be treated as purely literary,
quite uncontaminated by stage history. But we do not know
at what point they joined that history (the relationship of song-
texts to play-texts is everywhere obscure and little understood).
Clearly, the taste represented by these 'interpolations' or 'contributions' is unique in F, and no argument has so far been produced
to explain why these Purcellian or baroque accents appear in
contradiction of the 'Shakespearian' music audible elsewhere
in *Macbeth*. It still seems best, therefore, not to rewrite the
Folio text in order to accommodate them.

COLLATIONS

I.I

    8–9 1. I come, *Gray-Malkin.*
            All. Padock calls anon: faire is foule, and foule is
            faire

I.2

      0 *King Duncan, Malcolm*] *King Malcome*
    14 quarrel] Quarry
    45 *Exit Captain with Attendants*] *not in* F
    58 point-rebellious,] Point, rebellious (*most editors:*
          point rebellious,)

I.3

   96–7 as hail | Came] as Tale | Can (*Johnson:* as tale |
          Came)
   126 *They walk apart*] *not in* F

I.4

      0 *King Duncan, Lennox*] *King, Lenox*
     2 Are] Or

I.5

    15 human-kindness] humane kindnesse

I.6

      0 *King Duncan, Malcolm*] *King, Malcolme*
     9 most] must
    10 *Enter Lady Macbeth*] *Enter Lady*
    31 *He kisses her*] *not in* F

I.7

6 shoal] Schoole
28 *Enter Lady Macbeth*] *Enter Lady*
66 a-fume] a Fume (*other editors follow this F reading*)

II.1

30 *Exit Banquo and Fleance*] *Exit Banquo*
55 strides] sides
56 sure] sowre
57 way they] they may

II.2

0 *Enter Lady Macbeth*] *Enter Lady*
8 MACBETH (*within*)] *Enter Macbeth*
13 *Enter Macbeth, carrying two bloodstained daggers*]
   not in F
63 green one red] Greene one, Red
   Enter Lady Macbeth] *Enter Lady*

II.3

19 *He opens the gate*] *not in* F
39 *Enter Macbeth*] F *places after* 38
70 *Exeunt Macbeth and Lennox*] F *places after* awake
77 *Enter Lady Macbeth*] *Enter Lady*
122 *Lady Macbeth is taken out*] *not in* F
131 *Exeunt all but Malcolm and Donalbain*] *Exeunt*

III.1

11 *Lady Macbeth, Lennox*] *Lady Lenox*
44 *Exeunt Lords and Lady Macbeth*] *Exeunt Lords*
69 seeds] *as in* F (*most editors:* seed)
139 *Exeunt Murderers*] *not in* F
141 *Exit*] *Exeunt*

III.3

16 *They attack Banquo*] *not in* F
18 *Banquo falls. Fleance escapes*] *not in* F

III.4

0 *Lady Macbeth, Ross*] *Lady, Rosse*
4 *He walks around the tables*] *not in* F
12 *He rises and goes to the Murderer*] *not in* F
38 *Enter the Ghost of Banquo and sits in Macbeth's
   place*] F *places after* it (36)
72 *Exit Ghost*] *not in* F

106 *Exit Ghost*] *not in* F
143 in deed] indeed

III.6

24 son] Sonnes
38 the] their

IV.1

43 *Exeunt Hecat and the other three Witches*] *not in* F
58 germens] Germaine
92 Birnan] Byrnam
96 Rebellious dead] *as in* F (*most editors*: Rebellion's
    head)
105 *Hautboys*] F *places after* this
110 *and Banquo; the last king*] *and Banquo last*,

IV.2

79 *Enter Murderers*] F *places after* faces
83 shag-haired] shagge-ear'd
84 *He stabs him*] *not in* F
85 *Son dies. Exit Wife crying 'Murder'*] *Exit crying*
    Murther

IV.3

4 down-fallen] downfall
15 deserve] discerne
133 thy] they
145 *Exit Doctor*] F *places after* amend
234 tune] time

V.1

18 *Enter Lady Macbeth*] *Enter Lady*

V.3

19 *Exit Servant*] *not in* F
21 chair . . . dis-seat] cheere . . . dis-eate
39 Cure her] Cure
55 senna] Cyme
60 *Exit*] *not in* F
62 *Exit*] *Exeunt*

V.5

5 farced] forc'd
7 *A cry within of women*] F *places after* noise
8 *Exit*] *not in* F
15 *Enter Seyton*] *not in* F

v.6

10 F *marks a new scene at this point*
73 *Exit Macduff*] *not in* F

'Mislineation' in Macbeth

'Mislineation' is the name given to a printing of verse-lines
in a form which seems to the most experienced readers to run
counter to the author's usual procedure, requiring the modern
editor to relineate the verse (there is an elaborate discussion
of the topic in Brooke's edition, Appendix A). A fairly obvious
example occurs in *Macbeth* I.4.23–8, which appears in F as
follows:

Macb. The seruice, and the loyaltie I owe, |
In doing it, payes it selfe.
Your Highnesse part, | is to receiue our Duties:
And our Duties | are to your Throne, and State,
Children, and Seruants; | which doe but what they should,
By doing euery thing | safe toward your Loue
And Honor.
King. Welcome hither: |

Editors normally reline this, the new line-ends coming at the
points where I have inserted the vertical strokes. The reasons
which lie behind their efforts are both aesthetic and arithmetical. The lines as printed run oddly and clumsily; the sense-
rhythms contradict the verse-rhythms quite arbitrarily. Moreover,
it can be noticed that the completion of the half-line, with
subsequent division into full lines, produces a neat metrical
ending (a single and complete line of verse). The sum adds
up. But no more than arithmetical regularity would have been
achieved, if the sense-rhythms had not also been made to run
more easily; since they do so here, this may be taken as a
confirmation of the propriety of the relineation.

The difficulty of recognizing mislineation in Shakespeare is
usually greater than this. There is no necessity for his lines
to run with complete regularity; and certainly there is no rule
that interjections or new speeches should run to the end of

the line (on this matter, see Fredson Bowers, 'Establishing Shakespeare's Text: Notes on Short Lines and the Problems of Verse Division', *Studies in Bibliography* 33 (1980), pp. 74–130). Shakespeare wrote his plays to be spoken rather than written and no doubt thought of his rhythmic units in terms of the voice rather than the page. The editor is not dealing with material which aspires towards any single and definite printed form. This is particularly obvious when the editor has to deal with problems of verse or prose. It hardly helps here to know that Shakespeare did not think in terms of 'Now I'll write in prose', 'I think I'll write a few lines in verse here', but moved effortlessly all the way along a scale from the most rhythmical to the least rhythmical units. Conversations like that between young Macduff and his mother (IV.2), mainly in short units, raise really insoluble editorial problems when lines of the conversation fall into fairly obvious blank-verse units: *Thou speak'st with all thy wit*, says Macduff's wife, *And yet, i'faith, with wit enough for thee* (43–4). Is this verse or prose? The proper answer is 'Neither; it is speech'. F prints this example as verse, perhaps for no very good reason; and I have been content to follow it; but most editors have changed it to prose.

Macbeth is a play with a great deal of mislineation; and it is often suggested that this proves that it was rewritten or otherwise cut about. A number of reasons for this emerge, however, which have nothing to do with revision or rewriting. F is printed in double columns, on a narrower allowance of space for long lines than in modern editions. This leads to a number of what may be called 'normal' mislineations. The end of II.2 is printed in two passages of half-lines instead of whole lines (65–9 and 73, 74) partly to leave space for the *Knock* and *Exeunt* stage directions on the right-hand side of the column. I.3.77 is similarly divided into two, to allow space for the stage direction *Witches vanish*.

These are considerations which apply to all the plays; but there are further considerations which narrow the field of enquiry. The plays which Greg's *Shakespeare First Folio* mentions as posing particular problems of lineation are *Antony and Cleopatra*, *Timon of Athens* and *Coriolanus*. Add *Macbeth* to these and we have a probably almost complete list of the plays that Shakespeare wrote between 1606 and 1608. The verse of these plays has in common a new looseness of structure or fluidity of movement, and this may have imposed on either Shakespeare *or* the transcriber *or* the compositors (or all three) problems of conveying the 'feel' of the verse on to the page. Certainly there is evidence that F's compositors found it difficult to handle their material. The rhetoric of reported action, as it appears in *Macbeth*, has an individual rhythmic character, including a formal use of quasi-Virgilian short lines (*Till he faced the slave*, *I cannot tell*, *And fan our people cold*, *Craves composition*, *My liege*) which seems to have confused the compositor of I.2 and I.4, as it confuses modern editors. Again the fragmentary whispered conversation of II.2 in the style of

LADY

  Did not you speak?

MACBETH   When?

LADY   Now.

MACBETH   As I descended?

imposed its own problems, and produced its own crop of irregularities. It is worth noticing that the Witch scenes, with their clearly marked short lines, yield hardly any examples of mislineation.

    The difficulties of the compositors printing *Macbeth* did not arise solely from the rhetorical complexities of the verse but also from the technique of printing employed, no doubt aggravated here by complex line-structures. We now know that F was not printed in a simple sequence of pages but simultaneously at different parts of the book – see Charlton Hinman, *The Printing and Proof-reading of the First Folio of Shakespeare* (1963). In order to achieve this, the 'copy' which the printers used had to be marked off in approximate page-lengths, so that when printer A met up with printer B the material would join neatly without gaps or overlaps. The printed form had to be manipulated to fill the space of a page even if the material turned out to be too great or too little. When there was

too little material, the compositor would take to 'losing space'
by printing in short lines. When he was 'saving space' he
joined up lines. Several examples of this seem to be shown
in *Macbeth*. The second column of p. 136 in F, containing the
first forty-seven lines of II.2, is jammed full of type. Lines
like *I had most need of Blessing, and Amen stuck in my throat*
are pushed right up to the edge of the page. It seems obvious
that the compositor is saving space. The same seems to be
true on the first page of *Macbeth* in F (I.1 and I.2.1–65).

On the other hand the first column of p. 133 (I.3.105–56)
is very spaciously laid out, partly by the device of printing
several of the lines in two parts. The compositor clearly was
arranging to have the heading for scene 4 at the head of his
second column and was prepared to 'misline' to get it there.
Other fairly clear examples of 'space-losing' occur on F
p. 138 (II.3.70–II.4.19) and in the second column of p. 145
(IV.2.31–85).

I give below a full list of mislineations which have been
emended in this edition. The alternative version comes from
F. The end of the line in the F version is marked by a vertical
stroke preceded by the last word of the line; the spelling of
F has been preserved; but Elizabethan typographical conven-
tions have been normalized to accord with modern practice.
The layout is necessarily curt and even cryptic, but the interested reader should be able to reconstruct what has happened
in each case and see how far the mislineations fit into the
categories outlined above.

I.2

    33–5 Dismayed . . . lion] . . . *Banquoh* | . . . Eagles |
        . . . Lyon |
    38, 39 So . . . foe] *one line*
    42, 43 I cannot . . . help] . . . faint | . . . helpe |

I.3

      5 And . . . I] And mouncht, & mouncht, and
        mouncht | . . . I |
      77 With . . . you] . . . greeting | . . . you |
      81 Melted . . . stayed] . . . Winde | . . . stay'd |
    107, 108 The Thane . . . robes] . . . lives | . . . Robes |

110–13 Which he . . . know not] . . . loose | . . .
      Norway | . . . helpe | . . . labour'd | . . . not |
130, 131 Cannot . . . success] . . . good | . . . successe |
143 If . . . crown me] . . . King | . . . Crowne me |
149–53 Give . . . time] . . . favour | . . . forgotten | . . .
      registred | . . . Leafe | . . . them | . . . upon |
      . . . time |
156 Till . . . friends] . . . enough | . . . friends |

I.4

3–9 My liege . . . died] . . . back | . . . die | . . .
      hee | . . . Pardon | . . . Repentance | . . . him | . . .
      dy'de |
24–8 In doing . . . honour] . . . selfe | . . . Duties | . . .
      State | . . . should | . . . Love | . . . Honor |

I.5

20, 21 And yet . . . have it] . . . winne | . . . cryes | . . .
      have it |

I.6

1, 2 This . . . itself] . . . seat | . . . it selfe |
17–20 Against . . . hermits] . . . broad | . . . House | . . .
      Dignities | . . . Ermites |

II.1

4 Hold . . . heaven] . . . Sword | . . . Heaven |
7–9 And yet . . . repose] . . . sleepe | . . . thoughts |
      . . . repose |
16, 17 By . . . content] . . . Hostesse | . . . content |
25, 26 If you . . . for you] . . . consent | . . . for you |

II.2

2–6 What . . . possets] . . . fire | . . . shriek'd | . . .
      good-night | . . . open | . . . charge | . . .
      Possets |
14 I . . . noise] . . . deed | . . . noyse |
18, 19 Hark . . . chamber] *one line*
22–5 There's . . . to sleep] . . . sleepe | . . . other | . . .
      Prayers | . . . to sleepe |
32, 33 I had . . . throat] *one line*
65–9 To wear . . . more knocking] . . . white | . . .
      entry | . . . Chamber | . . . deed | . . .

Constancie | . . . unattended | . . . more
knocking |
73, 74   To know . . . couldst] . . . deed | . . . my selfe |
. . . knocking | . . . could'st |

II.3
22, 23   Faith . . . things] *two lines of verse*: . . . Cock |
. . . things |
48, 49   I'll . . . service] *one line*
51–3   The night . . . death] . . . unruly | . . . downe |
. . . Ayre | . . . Death |
56–8   New-hatched . . . shake] . . . time | . . . Night |
. . . fevorous | . . . shake |
83, 84   O Banquo . . . murdered] *one line*
118–20   What . . . brewed] . . . here | . . . hole | . . .
away | . . . brew'd |
132   What . . . them] . . . doe | . . . them |
134–8   Which . . . shot] . . . easie | . . . England | . . .
I | . . . safer | . . . Smiles | . . . bloody | . . .
shot |

II.4
14   And . . . certain] . . . Horses | . . . certaine |
19, 20   They . . . Macduff] . . . did so | . . . upon't |
. . . good *Macduffe* |

III.1
34, 35   Craving . . . with you] . . . Horse | . . . Night |
. . . with you |
41–5   Till . . . pleasure] . . . societie | . . . welcome |
. . . alone | . . . with you | . . . men | . . .
pleasure |
47–50   Bring . . . dares] . . . us | . . . thus | . . . deepe |
. . . that | . . . dares |
71   And . . . there] . . . th'utterance | . . . there |
74–81   Well then . . . might] . . . then | . . . speeches |
. . . past | . . . fortune | . . . selfe | . . .
conference | . . . you | . . . crost | . . . them |
. . . might |
84–90   I did . . . ever] . . . so | . . . now | . . .
meeting | . . . predominant | . . . goe | . . .
man | . . . hand | . . . begger'd | . . . ever |

113, 114 Both . . . enemy] *one line*
    127 Your . . . most] . . . you | . . . most |

III.2

    16 But . . . suffer] . . . dis-joint | . . . suffer |
    22 In . . . grave] . . . extasie | . . . Grave |
  32, 33 Unsafe . . . streams] . . . lave | . . . streames |
  43, 44 Hath . . . note] . . . Peale | . . . note |

III.3

    17 O . . . fly, fly, fly] . . . Trecherie | . . . flye, flye, flye |

III.4

  1, 2 You . . . welcome] . . . downe | . . . welcome |
  12, 13 The table . . . face] *one line*
  15, 16 My lord . . . him] *one line*
  19, 20 Most . . . perfect] . . . Sir | . . . scap'd | . . . againe | . . . perfect |
    47 Here . . . highness] . . . Lord | . . . Highnesse |
108, 109 You have . . . disorder] . . . mirth | . . . disorder |
   121 It . . . blood will have blood] . . . say | Blood will have Blood |

III.5

    36 Come . . . again] . . . be | . . . againe |

III.6

    1 My . . . thoughts] . . . Speeches | . . . Thoughts |

IV.1

    70 Macbeth, Macbeth, Macbeth . . . Macduff] *Macbeth, Macbeth, Macbeth* | . . . *Macduffe* |
    78 Be . . . scorn] . . . resolute | . . . scorne |
  85, 86 What . . . king] *one line*

IV.2

    27 Fathered he is . . . fatherless] Father'd he is | . . . Father-lesse |
  35, 36 Poor . . . gin] . . . Bird | . . . Lime | . . . Gin |
    37 Why . . . set for] . . . Mother | . . . set for |
    39 Yes . . . father] . . . dead | . . . Father |
  59, 60 Now . . . father] *verse:* . . . Monkie | . . . Father |
    79 To say . . . faces] . . . harme | . . . faces |

IV.3

    25 Perchance . . . doubts] . . . there | . . . doubts |

102, 103 Fit . . . miserable] *one line*

173, 174 Dying . . . grief] . . . sicken | . . . true | . . .
        griefe |

  211–13 My children . . . killed too] . . . Children too |
        . . . found | . . . kil'd too |

V.1

  44, 45 Go to, go to . . . not] Go too, go too | . . . not |
V.6

    1 Now . . . down] . . . enough | . . . downe |

    93 Hail . . . stands] . . . art | . . . stands |

Commentary

Biblical references are to the Bishops' Bible (1568, etc.), the version that was probably best known to Shakespeare.

I.1

'The true reason for the first appearance of the Witches is to strike the keynote of the character of the whole drama' (Coleridge).

3 *hurly-burly*: Confused turmoil.

4 *lost and won*: This is purposefully equivocal. When *Fair is foul* (9), losing may count as winning.

8 *Grey-Malkin*, *Padock*: These are the 'familiars' or demon-companions of the Witches. The usual identification of the first and second familiars with a cat and a toad is not fully confirmed by IV.1.1–3, and must be left undecided.

Anon: Soon. The Third Witch replies to her (unnamed) familiar.

10 *Hover*: This may be taken to imply that the Witches depart by flying.

I.2

The bleeding sergeant – himself an effective symbol of the battle he describes, and of Macbeth's part therein – speaks the inflated language suitable to his function as a passionate and weighty messenger. The *Alarum* at the beginning of the scene should form a natural bridge between the *filthy air* of the Witches' exit and the blood-daubed human being who staggers in from their *hurly-burly*.

3 *sergeant*: A word of three syllables. The rank is not
   that of the modern NCO but of an officer who is
   called *Captain* in the stage direction.

9 *choke their art*: Make impossible the art of swim-
   ming.

10 *to that*: As if to that end.

11–12 *multiplying villainies . . . Do swarm upon him*: Hosts
   of rebels join him like noxious insects swarming.

12 *Western Isles*: Hebrides.

13 *kerns and galloglasses*: Light- and heavy-armed Celtic
   levies.

16 *that name*: 'Brave'.

20 *the slave*: Macdonwald.

21 *ne'er shook hands nor bade farewell to him*: Engaged
   in none of the courtesies (or decencies) of war.

22 *nave to the chops*: Navel to the jaws.

24 *cousin*: This is a general term of kinship; but accurate (in the modern sense) here.

25 *reflection*: Turning-back at the vernal equinox.

26 *thunders*: The rhythm of the line is very often pieced-
   out by adding a verb ('break' is the favourite). But
   both rhythm and syntax work by suspension; the
   discord is not resolved till we reach *come* in the
   following line.

30 *skipping*: Lightly armed (perhaps also with the sense
   of 'footloose', 'light in allegiance').

31 *Norweyan*: The sources say 'Danish'. It has been
   suggested that Shakespeare changed this to avoid
   giving offence to Christian IV, King of Denmark
   (1577–1648).
   surveying vantage: Seeing his chance.

36 *say sooth*: Tell the truth.

38 *So they*: This short line, in the manner of Virgil, is
   used (like the epic simile) to mark the heroic tech-
   nique of the messenger's speech.

41 *memorize another Golgotha*: Make another field of the
   dead as memorable as Calvary.

48 *seems to*: Shows he is going to.

53 *Norway*: The King of Norway.

56 *Bellona's bridegroom*: Macbeth, fit husband for the goddess of war.

    lapped in proof: Clad in tested armour.

57 *him*: The King of Norway.

    self-comparisons: (1) In terms of bravery; (2) (ironically) in terms of treason.

58 *Point against point-rebellious, arm*: F reads *Point, rebellious*; most editors suppose that this makes *rebellious* qualify *arm*. I take the comma to be here (as often) equivalent to the modern hyphen, so that the first phrase means 'sword raised against rebellious sword'.

59 *lavish*: Excessive, ill-disciplined.

62 *composition*: Truce, agreement.

64 *Saint Colm's Inch*: Inchcolm (in the Firth of Forth).

70 *What he hath lost . . . won*: Note the ironic assimilation of the past traitor, Cawdor, and the future traitor, Macbeth.

I.3

This climatic scene brings together the thesis and antithesis of the first two scenes – the withered sisters and the blood-soaked soldiers. It reveals the quality of Macbeth's nature and contrasts that of Banquo; but it leaves the future open and ambiguous.

2 *Killing swine*: The bloodiest of domestic slaughterings.

6 *Aroint thee*: Begone.

    ronyon: A term of abuse particularly applied to fat women.

7 *Tiger*: This was an actual ship that sailed to Aleppo in 1583; it was in the London news in 1606. It sailed from England on 5 December 1604 and arrived back after fearful experiences on 27 June 1606. If we call the time away 568 days, this would be close enough to the *Weary sev'n-nights nine times nine* (22) that the Witches calculate (567 days).

9 *without a tail*: Impersonation by witchcraft was liable to deficiencies of this kind.

10 *do*: As in the modern vague abusive 'I'll do him' = 'I'll cause him harm'.

15 *the very ports they blow*: The winds blow *from* the ports, so that it is impossible to enter them.

16 *quarters*: Directions.

17 *Card*: Compass.

18–23 *I'll drain him dry as hay . . . peak, and pine*: Though ostensibly about the master of the *Tiger*, this serves as an accurate forecast of the fate of Macbeth. But 24–5 indicate an alternative ending to the story.

20 *penthouse*: A lean-to shed (his eyelids, oppressed by sleep, will slope over his eyes like the roof of a penthouse).

23 *peak*: Grow thin and sharp-featured.

31 *Weird Sisters*: 'Wyrd' is the Anglo-Saxon word for fate and *Weird* (noun) is the medieval and (later) northern form for one of the three Fates or Destinies – sometimes called the *Weird Sisters*. This was the nomenclature that Shakespeare inherited, but subsequent use of the phrase has been largely affected by *Macbeth*. Variant F spellings *weyward* and *weyard* may provide clues to Shakespeare's pronunciation.

32 *Posters*: Travellers.

37 *So foul and fair a day*: Catching up the *Fair is foul* exit of the Witches in I.1; so that, on entering, Macbeth seems to be entering into *their* world, in mind as well as body.

38 *is't called*: Is it said to be; is it.

43 *choppy*: Chapped, and so rough. The Witches lay their fingers to their lips, presumably to indicate the secret or forbidden nature of their communication.

47–9 *All hail*: It is worth noticing that Shakespeare elsewhere (*Richard II*, IV.1.169) associates this phrase with Judas's betrayal of Christ.

47 *Glamis*: It appears (I.5.13 and elsewhere) that Shakespeare used a two-syllable pronunciation of this word, 'Gla-miss', rather than the modern 'Glams'.

50–51 *Good sir . . . so fair*: Note the pun on *fear* and *fair* (pronounced alike in Shakespeare's day).

52 *fantastical*: Imaginary.

69 *imperfect*: Insufficiently explicit.

70 *Sinell*: A name for Macbeth's father.

71 *The Thane of Cawdor lives*: Evidently Macbeth does not know that the Thane of Cawdor has been assisting Norway.

83 *the insane root*: Any root that makes insane those who eat it.

91–2 *His wonders and his praises . . . his*: If he expresses his wonder (is dumbfounded) he cannot convey your praises. If he praises you he cannot express his own wonder (by being dumb).

103 *earnest*: Pledge.

a greater honour: Presumably Ross is only trying to convey Duncan's hyperbolic promises. But Macbeth (and the audience) are bound to think of the third prophecy.

111 *line*: Support.

rebel: Macdonwald.

119 *home*: All the way.

127 *swelling Act*: Magnificent theatrical experience.

129 *soliciting*: Allurement. This is not really true: the Witches do not allure, they simply present; but Macbeth's mind sees their words as allurement.

130 *Cannot be ill, cannot be good*: A subjective equivalent to *Fair is foul*.

133 *suggestion*: Prompting or incitement to evil.

134 *horrid*: Literally, 'bristling' (like the *hair*).

136–7 *Present fears . . . imaginings*: Frightful things in the present have less effect on us than imagined horrors.

138 *fantastical*: Imaginary.

139 *single*: Individual (sometimes taken to mean 'weak').

140–41 *function is smothered . . . is not*: The power to act is annihilated by my speculations; so that the only thing that exists in the present is what does not really exist in the present – thoughts of the future.

146 *Come what come may*: Whatever happens.

147 *Time and the hour runs through the roughest day*: Whatever is going to happen *will* happen, inevitably.

149–50 *My dull brain . . . things forgotten*: Macbeth excuses his inattention by the lie that his mind is caught up in things of the past. In fact, it is caught up in the future.

155 *free hearts*: Open feelings.

I.4

The first Cawdor's good end is played against the second Cawdor's bad beginning. The court of Duncan is revealed as a family unit, bound by natural ties of trust and loyalty. The naming of the heir, which might have given the historical Macbeth a legitimate cause to supplant the King, is here brought forward without this political consequence; it merely isolates Macbeth from the national life, drives him further into the world of his imagination.

10 *had been studied*: Had learned his part in the play.

11 *owed*: Owned.

15 *O worthiest cousin*: Note the ironic turn from Cawdor, as a traitorous hypocrite, to Macbeth.

17 *before*: In advance of my power of repayment.

20 *proportion both of thanks and payment*: The weighing up how much was due and how much should be paid.

21–2 *Only I have left . . . all can pay*: All that I have to pay you with is the statement that I cannot repay you.

23–4 *The service . . . pays itself*: The reward for service and loyalty is found in the joy of doing loyal acts of service.

25–8 *and our duties . . . toward your love and honour*: Our duties to your throne only express their nature as absolute dependants when they are doing everything possible to protect you.

37 *you whose places are the nearest*: The next nearest to the throne (after the *Sons, kinsmen, thanes*).

38 *estate*: State, kingdom.

45 *The rest is labour, which is not used for you*: It is wearisome to be inactive, when we know we ought to be doing something to serve you.

46 *harbinger*: Officer sent ahead of the king to arrange his lodgings.

53 *wink*: Keep shut.

let that be: May the action come into being.

I.5

The violent certainty of Lady Macbeth acts as a catalyst to crystallize a mode of action and of character-development out of the uncertainties of previous scenes. At the same time a new and more intimate image of Macbeth emerges to complicate what we have known and guessed at.

15 *human-kindness*: The quality of creatureliness, or humanity, that he sucked from his mother; what binds the individual to the social order of Man. (There is no evidence that Lady Macbeth has to fear the *kindness* – in the ordinary modern sense – of Macbeth's nature.)

18 *illness*: Wickedness.

highly: Greatly.

21 *That which cries . . . have it*: The ambitious ends proposed cry out for immoral action on the part of anyone who hopes to achieve them.

22 *that*: The end which Macbeth *wouldst . . . have*.

24 *That I may pour my spirits in thine ear*: As Claudius poisoned the elder Hamlet.

27 *metaphysical*: Supernatural.

35 *tending*: Attendance.

36 *raven*: Messenger of death.

37 *fatal*: To Duncan.

39 *mortal thoughts*: Murderous designs.

unsex: Take away my feminine qualities.

41 *Make thick my blood*: 'So that pity cannot flow along her veins and reach her heart' (Bradley).

44–5 *keep peace between . . . it*: Act as a restraining influence, and so impede the translation of purpose into effect.

46 *take my milk for gall*: 'Take away my milk and put gall into the place' (Dr Johnson).

murdering ministers: Agents of murder (the *spirits* of 38).

47 *sightless*: Invisible.

48 *wait on nature's mischief*: Accompany natural disasters.

49 *pall thee*: Wrap yourself.

53 *the all-hail hereafter*: The third *All hail* with which the Witches greeted Macbeth (I.3.49) prophesied that he should become King. Lady Macbeth refers to this future state.

61–2 *To beguile . . . the time*: To deceive people look as they expect you to look.

70 *favour*: Face, appearance.

I.6

The final calm before the storm. In immediate contrast to the enclosed darkness of the previous scene is the open, light naturalness of this one. The elaboration of Lady Macbeth's rhetoric is a symptom of her falsity.

0 *Hautboys and torches*: Are these needed in this daylight scene? Perhaps the attendants who normally perform these functions are meant.

1 *seat*: Situation.

1–3 *the air . . . our gentle senses*: The air is prompt to come forward and show its merits.

3 *gentle senses*: Perhaps 'the senses which the air greets like gentlemen' or simply 'our refined sensibilities'.

4 *temple-haunting martlet*: The martin, commonly building its nest in churches.
approve: Prove.

5 *his loved mansionry*: His love of building.

6 *jutty*: Projection.

7 *coign of vantage*: Advantageous corner.

9 *haunt*: Frequent.

11–14 *The love that follows us . . . trouble*: I have followed you to Inverness. This indicates my love; yet it is also troublesome. However, in such situations we tend to think of the love and ignore the trouble. By saying this I have taught you how to pray for the good of those who trouble you.

13 *bid*: Pray.

16 *single*: Slight, trivial.

20 *We rest your hermits*: We remain bound to pray for you.

22 *purveyor*: Officer sent in advance, to obtain food for the main party.

26–8 *in compt . . . to return your own*: Macbeth and his Lady are only the stewards of their possessions; they are ready to account for them and render them up whenever Duncan, the real owner, requires.

I.7

This scene is the climax of Act I, with the order and the disorder themes brought into sharpest opposition. The opening dumb-show of feasting must create a context of trust and benevolence around Macbeth's soliloquy and the dialogue that follows, so as to keep the argument for society before our eyes while (with our minds) we see the individual move towards his great betrayal.

0 *Sewer*: Superintendent of the feast.

1 *If it were done when 'tis done*: If the doing of the deed were the end of it.

3 *trammel up the consequence*: Catch up (as in a net) the trail of consequences that follows any action. (The metaphor is continued in *catch | With his surcease success*.)

4 *With his surcease*: Either (1) by Duncan's death or (2) by putting an end to the consequences. Shakespeare regularly uses *his* for modern 'its'.
that but: So that only.

6 *bank and shoal*: F's *Banke and Schoole* can be seen simply as an older spelling of the version printed here – the sense being that time is only an isthmus between two eternities. On the other hand, *bank* often means 'bench', and the train of words *bank . . . school . . . judgement . . . teach* seems significant.

7 *jump the life to come*: Hazard things outside the scope of here-and-now.

8 *that*: In that.

10 *even-handed justice*: Precise retribution. The lines which follow forecast the exact nature of Macbeth's

fate – by destroying trust he destroys his own capacity for trust.

11 *ingredience*: Composition.

poisoned chalice: The chalice is a particularly treacherous vehicle of murder, being (like Macbeth's castle) the vessel of sacredness and trust.

17 *faculties*: Powers.

18 *clear*: Spotless.

22 *Striding the blast*: Astride the storm (of indignation).

22–3 *heaven's cherubin, horsed . . . the air*: Probably suggested by Psalm 18:10: 'He rid upon the Cherub and he did flee; he came fleeing upon the wings of the wind.' The *sightless* (invisible) *curriers* (runners) are the winds in motion. The baby *Pity*, and the baby-like *cherubin* (Shakespearian form of Hebrew '*Cherubim*'), will ride on the winds and *blow* the deed like dust into *every eye*, so that everyone will know it, and weep (1) because of the dust; (2) because of pity.

23 *curriers*: I have preserved this form (1) to avoid the inappropriate connotations of the modern 'courier'; (2) to keep the short vowel-sound of the Elizabethan form, in a line requiring (because of the sense) to be made up of short sounds. F reads *Curriors*.

25 *That tears shall drown the wind*: 'Alluding to the remission of the wind in a shower' (Dr Johnson).

25–8 *I have no spur . . . the other*: The horse imagery of *Striding* and *horsed* leads now (1) to a view of Macbeth's intention to murder as a horse that must be spurred, and (2) to a view of ambition (which could be a *spur* or stimulus) as a rider *vaulting* into his saddle, but overshooting the mark and falling on the other side.

28 *the other*: The other side.

Enter Lady Macbeth: Sometimes seen as an ironic answer to Macbeth's *I have no spur*.

32 *bought*: By his bravery in battle.

34 *in their newest gloss*: The *Golden opinions* are seen as new suits of clothes.

37 *green and pale*: Nauseated, as in the morning after drunkenness.

39 *Such*: As drunken lechery.

41-2 *that . . . ornament of life*: Greatness, the crown.

44 *wait upon*: Accompany.

45 *the adage*: The proverb 'the cat wanted to eat fish, but would not wet her feet'.

46-7 *I dare do all . . . none*: To be daring is manly; but to be too daring may carry one right outside the limits proper to human (and humane) activity. Lady Macbeth's reply is that a man deficient in continued daring is a *beast*. To exceed in daring is to exceed in manliness. She chooses to ignore the question of humanity.

48 *break this enterprise to me*: Presumably she refers to the letter she reads above, so that what she says is not literally true; but Lady Macbeth is persuading, not recounting, and neither she nor Shakespeare is bound to literal truth.

53 *They have made themselves*: Duncan is now in our power.

that their fitness: That fitness of theirs (fitness of time and place for the murder).

54 *unmake you*: Make you incapable.

59-61 *We fail . . . we'll not fail*: Lady Macbeth's reply is printed in F as a question – but the question mark then served also for the exclamation mark. If she scornfully repeats Macbeth's question, then *But* must mean 'only'. If (with an exclamation mark) she accepts the possibility of failure, *But* is the usual disjunctive. I have preferred the latter interpretation.

60 *screw your courage to the sticking place*: The metaphor is from the cross-bow, in which the *sticking place* was the notch into which the string fitted when sufficiently 'screwed up'.

63 *chamberlains*: Attendants on the bed-chamber.

64 *wassail*: Festivity.

convince: Overcome.

65 *the warder of the brain*: Memory guards us against

the performance of deeds that proved shameful in
the past.

66–7 *receipt of reason . . . limbeck only*: The part of the
brain where reasons are received or collected will
be a retort or alembic, full of the fumes that accompany distillation.

68 *drenchèd*: Drenched with drink.

71 *spongy officers*: The drink-sodden chamberlains.

72 *quell*: Murder.

72–4 *Bring forth men-children . . . Nothing but males*:
Macbeth accepts and endorses his wife's version of
'manliness'.

74 *received*: By the minds of observers.

79–80 *bend up . . . corporal agent*: Strain every muscle.

81 *mock the time*: Macbeth repeats his wife's advice to
beguile the time (I.5.61).

II.1

Just before the fatal deed Banquo is reintroduced
beside Macbeth to highlight the central distinction
between a moral will and a moralizing imagination.

4 *husbandry*: Thrift (the heavens are 'husbanding' their
resources).

5 *Take thee that too*: '*That* is precisely what the actor
who plays Banquo hands to the actor (or actress)
who plays Fleance – "his dagger" in Booth's production; "his hat" in Phelps's' (Sprague).

14 *offices*: Servants' quarters.

16 *shut up*: Concluded his speech.

18 *Our will became the servant to defect*: Our desire (to
be hospitable) was bound in by the limitations
imposed by our unpreparedness.

25 *cleave to my consent when 'tis*: Adhere to my opinion
when we discuss the matter.

27–8 *keep . . . allegiance clear*: Keep my heart free from
evil, and my allegiance to the King untainted.

36 *fatal*: Ominous.
   sensible: Open to sensory apprehension.

42 *Thou marshall'st me . . . going*: The visionary dagger
seems to float before him and lead him (like a

'marshal' or usher) to the door of Duncan's bed-chamber.

44–5 *Mine eyes . . . worth all the rest*: Either the dagger does not exist, in which case the sight of it is false; or else the vision is of a higher truth than that of normal sense-experience.

46 *dudgeon*: Handle.

gouts: Drops.

48 *informs*: Makes shapes.

49 *half-world*: Hemisphere.

51 *curtained*: (1) Behind bed-curtains; (2) hidden from conscious control.

51–2 *Witchcraft celebrates* | *Pale Hecat's offerings*: Witchcraft celebrates its sacrificial rites to Hecat (goddess of the moon as well as of witches, and therefore *Pale*).

53 *Alarumed*: Aroused.

55 *Tarquin's ravishing strides*: The stealthy steps that Tarquin took while moving towards his rape of Lucrece.

58 *Thy very stones prate of my whereabout*: This is probably from Luke 19:40: 'if these hold their peace, then shall the stones cry.'

59 *take the present horror from the time*: Break the ghastly silence.

II.2

An ecstasy of moral hysteria follows the murder. The disjointed language suggests both guilt and terror, in a kind of hell cut off from humanity, till reawakened by the *knocking* at the end of the scene.

2 *quenched*: Made unconscious (by drink).

3 *fatal bellman*: The owl, as the bird of death, is compared to the bellman sent to give *stern'st good-night* to condemned prisoners the night before their execution.

5 *The doors are open*: (1) The physical impediments have been overcome; (2) moral restraints have been abolished.

grooms: Royal servants with specific household duties.

6 *mock their charge*: Make a mockery of their duty to guard the King.

possets: Restorative night-drinks.

7 *nature*: The forces of life.

13 *My husband*: The only time she uses this term.

20 *sorry sight*: We heard much about the loyally blood-stained Macbeth in I.2. The first time we *see* him blood-stained it is with the blood of his rightful King.

21 *A foolish thought, to say a sorry sight*: Lady Macbeth attempts a comforting jocularity: 'It would be foolish (or *sorry*) of you to feel sorrow for such a deed.'

22 *one did laugh . . . Murder*: Presumably Donalbain and his companion (Malcolm?) in the second chamber (also the *One* and *other* of 26).

27 *hangman's*: Bloody (because he dismembered as well as hanged).

30 *Consider*: Contemplate.

32 *most need of blessing*: Because he was falling into sin. Notice the avoidance of responsibility for his action.

34 *so*: If you do so.

37 *ravelled sleave*: Tangled skein.

38 *bath*: That which eases the hurt.

39 *second course*: (1) The most sustaining dish in the feast – the *Chief nourisher* (anciently, meat came in the second course); (2) the second mode of existence.

45 *unbend*: Dismantle.

47 *filthy witness*: The tell-tale blood.

54–5 *pictures . . . bleed*: Notice the stark contrast between these words. Lady Macbeth must be seen to be falsifying.

56–7 *I'll gild the faces of the grooms . . . their guilt*: The pun marks the tension of the moment; moreover, to Lady Macbeth '*guilt* is something like *gilt* – one can wash it off or paint it on' (Cleanth Brooks).

62 *multitudinous*: Multiform; or 'teeming with multitudes of creatures'.

incarnadine: Turn red.

63 *green one red*: Either 'green-one red' or 'green, one red'. Cf. Revelation 16:3: 'And the second angel shed out his vial upon the sea, and it turned as it were into the blood of a dead man.'

64 *My hands are of your colour*: From 'gilding' the faces of the chamberlains.

67 *A little water*: In strong contrast to *multitudinous seas* above.

71 *watchers*: Awake ('watch' is a variant form of 'wake').

73 *To know my deed 'twere best not know myself*: If I am to think about the murder I must stop being conscious of the man I have been.

II.3

This scene is sometimes thought un-Shakespearian because 'low'. But the Porter scene is a typically Elizabethan double-take of damnation and its precedents, based on the tradition of Estates-Satire, in which *some of all professions* (17) were surveyed and condemned. The Porter of hell-gate was a figure in the medieval drama, an opposite to St Peter, and opponent of Christ in 'the harrowing of Hell'. The faked business of the following 'council scene' (undercut by the asides of Malcolm and Donalbain) points forward to the emptiness of social gatherings under Macbeth.

0 *within*: Behind the stage façade (meaning *outside* in terms of stage illusion).

2 *old*: Plenty of (colloquial intensive).

4–5 *Here's a farmer . . . plenty*: The farmer stored his crops, hoping that prices would rise; when the next season produced an expectation of plentiful crops, prices fell and he hanged himself (the traditional expression of religious despair).

5 *Come in time*: This, the F reading, makes a weak kind of sense: 'Come in good time.' Dover Wilson's emendation to 'time-server' is attractive and apposite, but not necessary.

napkins: To mop up the sweat. Did the farmer hang himself in his napkin?

7 *the other devil*: The Porter wishes to mention some devil other than *Belzebub* (4), but cannot remember the name of any.

8 *equivocator*: Usually taken as a reference to the Jesuits, and especially to Father Garnet, who, in the Gunpowder Plot trial, 'equivocated', swore evidence with mental reservation that it was not true. But equivocation (by Witches, by Macbeth) runs throughout the whole play.

9–10 *treason enough for God's sake*: Presumably another reference to the Jesuit.

13–14 *stealing out of a French hose*: *hose* were breeches, which about the time of *Macbeth* changed fashion from wide to narrow (*French*) fitting. The tailor had been accustomed to steal cloth from the baggy breeches, but was detected in the closer-fitting ones.

14 *roast your goose*: (1) Heat your smoothing iron (*goose*); (2) ?'cook your goose' (undo yourself).

19 *I pray you remember the porter*: Returning to his role as the company clown, the Porter begs for a tip.

22–3 *second cock*: Three o'clock in the morning. (It is now daybreak.)

32–3 *equivocates him in a sleep*: Fulfils his lechery only in a dream.

33 *giving him the lie*: (1) Deceives him; (2) floors him; (3) makes him urinate (*lie* = lye).

37 *took up my legs*: As a wrestler lifts his opponent.

38 *cast*: (1) Throw (as in wrestling); (2) vomit.

43 *timely*: Early.

47 *The labour we delight in physics pain*: When we enjoy doing something, the enjoyment counters the laboriousness.

49 *limited*: Appointed.

52–6 *Our chimneys were blown down . . . woeful time*: Nature expresses the breach of natural order by 'natural' convulsions.

56 *New-hatched to the woeful time*: Newly emerged to make the time woeful.

obscure bird: The owl, bird of darkness, thought to portend death.

61 *Tongue . . . name thee*: Note the chiastic order: it is the heart which conceives, the tongue which names.

63 *Confusion*: Destruction.

65 *The Lord's anointed temple*: The temple (body) of the Lord's anointed (combining 2 Corinthians 6:16: 'ye [Christians] are the temple of the living God' and 1 Samuel 24:10: 'the Lord's anointed' – note the context of this latter passage).

69 *Gorgon*: She turned to stone those who looked on her.

75 *Great Doom's image*: A replica of the Last Judgement.

76 *As from your graves rise up*: Act as if at the Last Judgement itself, to fit in with the present horror (*countenance* is also used in the sense of 'behold').

77 *Ring the bell*: This is sometimes supposed to be a stage direction added by the prompter, and accidentally printed as part of the text.

79 *trumpet*: The trumpet is an appropriate metaphor for the bell, because of the Last Judgement atmosphere.

90 *mortality*: Human life.

92 *lees*: Dregs.

93 *vault*: (1) Wine vault; (2) sky.

94 *You are*: You are *amiss*, since you have lost your father.

99 *badged*: Marked.

107 *expedition*: Haste.

108 *pauser*: That should make one pause.

109 *His silver skin . . . golden blood*: 'Dressed in the most precious of garments, the royal blood itself' (Cleanth Brooks).

113 *Unmannerly breeched*: Wearing an improper (?inhuman) kind of breeches (the blood of the King, the man they should defend).

115 *swooning*: Critics dispute whether this is a genuine swoon (due to womanly exhaustion) or a ruse (designed to distract attention from her husband).

117 *argument*: Theme of discourse (here, the horror of Duncan's death).

119 *Hid in an auger-hole*: Concealed, by treachery, in the smallest crevice.

120 *brewed*: Matured.

121 *Nor our strong sorrow upon the foot of motion*: Our sorrow is stronger than shows at the moment; it has not yet begun to move, to take action.

123 *our naked frailties hid*: Clothed our poor, half-naked bodies (with a side-glance at the frailty of the whole human condition).

126 *scruples*: Doubts.

127 *In the great hand of God I stand*: I put myself at God's disposal (to be compared with Macbeth's appeal for *manly readiness* below).
    thence: Relying on God.

128 *undivulged pretence*: Purpose as yet unrevealed.

130 *put on manly readiness*: Put on clothes *and* resolute minds.

137–8 *The nea'er in blood . . . bloody*: The more closely related people are, the more likely they are to try to murder us.

140 *the aim*: The beginning of the purpose.

141 *dainty of*: Particular about.

142–3 *There's warrant . . . no mercy left*: In these circumstances to steal away is a justified kind of stealing.

II.4

This scene serves to slow down the time movement and to withdraw the camera from the agonizing close-ups of the preceding episodes. The Old Man here is a choric figure, imported to give a view of the action from outside, and to show it in large-scale perspective. The natural portents take their place in this perspective as expressing heaven's view of what has happened.

4 *trifled*: Made trivial.
  father: Old man.

5–6 *heavens . . . act . . . stage*: Theatrical terms.

7 *travelling lamp*: The sun.

12 *towering in her pride of place*: Circling to reach her highest pitch (technical terms of falconry).

13 *a mousing owl*: An owl whose nature it is to hunt close to the ground for mice, not for falcons.

15 *minions of their race*: The darlings of horse-breeding.

24 *pretend*: Intend.

suborned: Bribed to do evil.

28–9 *raven up . . . life's means*: Devour improvidently the sustenance (lineal respect, paternal love) on which their life and their own succession depended.

30 *sovereignty will fall upon Macbeth*: Macbeth was the next heir, Duncan and Macbeth both being grandsons, of the older and younger branches respectively, of Malcolm II, the previous king.

33 *Colmekill*: Iona (the burial-place of Scottish kings from 973 to 1040).

36 *Fife*: Macduff's own territory.

38 *Lest our old robes sit easier than our new*: The new monarch is likely to be more severe than the former one.

40–41 *God's benison go with you . . . friends of foes*: Blessed be the peacemakers.

III.1

After some time has elapsed we meet Macbeth again and note that he has developed into a very poised tyrant. The contrast with Banquo is one which he cannot now bear, and his new skill is shown in his organizing the means to remove his 'enemy'.

4 *stand in thy posterity*: Remain in your family.

7 *shine*: Are glowingly fulfilled.

10 *Sennet*: Flourish of trumpets to announce important entry.

15 *I'll*: Condescension from the royal *we* to the personal *I* to indicate special affability – shown also by *request*.

16 *to the which*: The antecedent to *which* is the idea of 'your commandment'.

17 *indissoluble*: Main stress on second syllable.

21 *still*: Always.

25 *the better*: Better than that.

32 *strange invention*: That Macbeth was the murderer.

33 *therewithal*: Besides that.

cause of state: State business.

42–3 *To make society the sweeter welcome . . . supper-time
      alone*: I will avoid company now so that it may be
      more pleasant when we meet again at supper.

47 *To be thus*: To be King.

48–9 *Our fears in Banquo | Stick deep*: Our fear of Banquo
      is like a thorn in our flesh.

49 *royalty of nature*: Natural regality of temper.

50 *that*: The *royalty*, a quality loftily independent of
   Macbeth's interests. Cf. Iago's 'He hath a daily beauty
   in his life | That makes me ugly' in *Othello*,
   V.1.19–20.

55 *genius*: Guardian spirit.
   it is said: By Plutarch, in the *Life of Antony*. Cf.
   Antony and Cleopatra, II.3.29–31: 'thy spirit | Is all
   afraid to govern thee near him; | But, he away, 'tis
   noble.'

61 *grip*: Editors usually print *gripe*, the F form. But
   there seems no case against modernizing; in this sense,
   the two forms of the word are indistinguishable.

62 *unlineal*: Not of my family.

64 *filed*: Defiled.

65 *gracious*: Filled with (religious) grace.

66 *Put rancours in the vessel of my peace*: Put irritants
   where there used to be peace. In view of the prevail-
   ingly religious tone of the context *vessel* may be the
   chalice and the whole phrase mean 'took me out of
   the state of grace'.

67 *eternal jewel*: Immortal soul.

68 *the common enemy of man*: The devil.

70–71 *come fate into the list . . . utterance*: Let fate enter
       the tournament and face me in a duel '*à outrance*',
       that is, to the death.

76–7 *held you . . . under fortune*: Kept you in a lowly
      condition.

79 *passed in probation*: Went over the proofs.

80 *borne in hand*: Kept in delusion.
   instruments: Agents.

82 *half a soul*: A halfwit.

83 *Banquo*: Notice how this essential information about

the name of the person being discussed is delayed
to the end of the speech.

87 *so gospelled*: So meekly Christian (as to 'love your
enemies . . . pray for them which hurt you and
persecute you' (Matthew 5:44)).

90 *yours*: Your family, your issue.

91–107 *Ay, in the catalogue ye go for men . . . perfect*: Macbeth
now uses the taunt of unmanliness which was so effective when used against him.

91 *catalogue*: An undiscriminating list (set in contrast
to the *valued file*).

93 *Shoughs*: Shaggy Icelandic dogs (probably pronounced to rhyme with 'lochs').
water-rugs: The name suggests that these are rough-
haired water-dogs.
demi-wolves: Cross-bred from dog and wolf.

94 *valued file*: The catalogue rearranged to show the
prices.

96 *house-keeper*: Domestic watchdog.

99–100 *Particular addition . . . all alike*: The *valued file* gives
back an individual title to each item, to discrimi-
nate it from the sameness of mere species, found in
the *bill*.

101–2 *file . . . rank*: Moving from the sense of *file* above
(94) to the military sense.

106 *in his life*: While he lives.

111 *tugged with*: Knocked about by.

112 *set*: Gamble.

115 *distance*: (1) Dissension; (2) space between combatants in fencing.

116–17 *every minute of his being . . . life*: His very existence
is like a sword thrusting against my vitals (picking
up second sense in *distance*, 115).

118 *With bare-faced power*: Using my power as King
quite openly.

119 *bid my will avouch it*: Justify it by my impulse.

120 *For*: For the sake of; on account of.

123 *I to your assistance do make love*: I woo your power
to come to my aid.

127 *Your spirits shine through you*: Say no more; I see
    your resolution in your eyes.

129 *the perfect spy o'the time*: Perhaps the Third Murderer
    (who appears in III.3); but may simply mean 'the perfect
    report (espial) on the time (to commit the murder)'.

131 *something*: Somewhat; some distance.
    thought: Be it understood.

132 *I require a clearness*: I must be able to clear myself
    of any suspicion.

133 *rubs nor botches*: Unevennesses; clumsy work.

137 *Resolve yourselves apart*: Go away and make up your
    minds.

III.2

    The development in Macbeth is shown in domestic
    as well as political relationship. He dominates his
    wife's conduct with eloquent restlessness. Note also
    the corresponding change in Lady Macbeth.

 4 *Naught's had, all's spent*: We have given everything,
   and achieved nothing.

 7 *by destruction dwell in doubtful joy*: Achieve, by
   destroying, only an apprehensive joy.

 9 *sorriest*: Most wretched.

10 *Using*: Keeping company with.

11 *them*: May imply a number of murders.

13 *scorched*: Slashed, as with a knife.

14 *close*: Join up again (as a worm does).

15 *former tooth*: Her fangs, as dangerous as they were
   before the 'scorching'.

16 *frame of things disjoint*: The whole structure of the
   universe go to pieces.
   both the worlds suffer: Terrestrial and celestial worlds perish.

20 *to gain our peace, have sent to peace*: We killed to
   gain peace of mind, but have only managed to give
   peace to our victims.

21 *the torture of the mind*: The bed is a rack.

22 *In restless ecstasy*: In a frenzy of delirium.

23 *fitful*: Marked by paroxysms or fits.

25 *foreign levy*: An army levied abroad.

27 *rugged*: Monosyllabic here.

30 *Let your remembrance apply*: Remember to pay special attention (*remembrance* has four syllables).

31 *Present him eminence*: Give him special honour.

32–3 *Unsafe the while . . . streams*: The time is so unsafe for us that we can only keep our honours clean by washing them in flattery. ('A grotesque and violent figure which shows the impatient self-contempt of the speaker' (Kittredge).)

34 *vizards*: False faces.

38 *nature's copy*: (1) The form that Nature has given them by copying the first creation: 'particular casts from Nature's mould'; (2) copyhold – a lease that can be broken.

40 *jocund*: Note how joy is associated with death.

41 *cloistered*: The bat flies in and around buildings rather than in the open air.

42 *shard-borne*: (1) Born in dung; (2) borne aloft by its wing-cases.

44 *note*: (1) Memory; (2) sound.

45 *dearest chuck*: A grim intimacy.

46–7 *Come, seeling night . . . pitiful day*: Night is to hide the dreadful deed from daylight as the falconer 'seels' or sews up the eyes of the hawk.

47 *Scarf up*: Blindfold.

48 *bloody and invisible*: The falconer's hand is *bloody* (from the *seeling*) and is *invisible* to the hawk, now effectively blinded.

49 *that great bond*: The moral law; or perhaps the sixth commandment, against killing. (Perhaps *bond* should be pronounced 'band', to rhyme with *hand*.)

50 *pale*: (1) Paled, fenced-in – following a secondary sense in *bond* (= bondage); (2) tender-hearted, a creature seeing through the *tender eye of pitiful day*.
thickens: Grows dense, opaque, dim.

53 *to their preys do rouse*: Bestir themselves to hunt their prey.

III.3

The altercation between the Third Murderer and the other two is a nice illustration of the dependence of tyranny on mistrust.

3 *offices*: Duties.

4 *To the direction just*: Exactly as required.

stand: 'Wait here'; or 'join our side'.

6 *lated*: Belated; overtaken by the night.

10 *within . . . expectation*: In the list of expected guests.

12–14 *he does usually.* | *So all . . . their walk*: F has a comma after *usually*, allowing one to phrase it *he does . . . (So all men . . .) make it their walk.*

16 *Let it come down*: Let 'the rain of blood' come down.

III.4

This scene gives the success and failure of Macbeth's assault on 'royalty' its climactic expression, and makes the contrast between false order and true order quite explicit. It should recall the earlier banquet which welcomed Duncan to Inverness (I.7) – a true image of kingly *content*; and it also looks forward to the inhuman banquet of the Witches in IV.1. The final episode, with the King and Queen abandoned and guilt-oppressed amid the relics of their feasting, gives eloquent visual expression to the meaning of their fates.

1 *degrees*: Rank, position at table. The feast is a symbol of order.

1–2 *At first* | *And last*: Once and for all.

2, 6, 8 *welcome*: 'The first three speeches of the King and Queen end with the word "welcome"' (Kittredge).

3 *mingle with society*: Leave the dais; move round among the guests.

5 *state*: Canopied throne.

in best time: When it is most appropriate.

9–10 *See, they encounter thee . . . even*: Perhaps some stage direction is necessary here to indicate the mode by which the guests show their *even* (equivalent) response to the Queen. On the other hand, the *even* is often taken to refer to the table: both sides are full, so *Here I'll sit i'the midst*.

18 *the nonpareil*: Without an equal.

20 *fit*: Fever of anxiety.

perfect: Completely secure, healthy.

21 *Whole*: Unbroken (in surface).
   founded: Secure.

22 *broad and general*: Wide-embracing.
   casing: Enveloping.

23 *cabined . . . bound in*: Imprisoned (the 'damnable iteration' conveys Macbeth's hysterical intensity).

24 *saucy*: Importunate.

24, 25 *safe*: Heavily ironic.

28 *worm*: Little serpent.

31 *hear ourselves*: Hear one another. (Notice the assimilation of the King and the Murderer.)

32 *give the cheer*: Welcome your guests.

32–4 *The feast is sold . . . with welcome*: It is merely a commercial affair if the hosts do not punctuate the feast with assertions of welcome.

34–5 *To feed were best at home . . . ceremony*: If feeding is the sole concern, home is the best place for it; away from home it is ceremony that makes a feast worthwhile (*ceremony*, pronounced 'seer-money', seems to have been trisyllabic in Shakespeare's day).

36 *remembrancer*: An officer whose original function was to remind his superior of his duties.

37 *good digestion wait on appetite*: Enjoy whatever you eat.

39 *our country's honour*: All the nobility of Scotland.

40 *graced*: (1) Our guest of honour; (2) full of grace.

41 *challenge for*: Reproach with.

48 *done this*: (1) Killed Banquo; (2) filled up the seat.

49 *Thou canst not say I did it*: Macbeth defends himself by saying that he did not strike the actual blow against Banquo.

54 *upon a thought*: In a moment.

59 *proper stuff*: Stuff and nonsense.

61 *air-drawn*: Sketched out of air; pulled through air.

62 *flaws*: Sudden gusts (of passion).

63–5 *Impostors to true fear . . . her grandam*: These are not concerned with reality, but are simply passions such as would be appropriate to a dramatic rendering of a ghost story – one whose credibility rests on the authority of an old woman.

65 *Authorized*: Accent on second syllable.

70–72 *If charnel-houses . . . maws of kites*: If the dead return from normal burial-places, we will have to throw their bodies for birds of prey to eat.

70 *charnel-houses*: Bone-stores.

75 *Ere humane statute purged the gentle weal*: Before the benevolence of law cleansed society and made it gentle.

80 *mortal murders*: Fatal wounds.

81 *push us from our stools*: (1) Occupy the seat at the feast; (2) take over the succession to the throne.

90 *we thirst*: We are anxious to drink.

91 *And all to all*: Let all men drink to everyone.
Our duties and the pledge: We drink our homage to you, and the toast you have just proposed.

94 *speculation*: Power of knowing what you see.

100 *armed*: Armour-plated.
Hyrcan: Tigers in Latin literature were often said to come from Hyrcania, by the Caspian Sea.

101 *nerves*: Sinews.

104 *If trembling I inhabit then*: If I live in a trembling body, if I harbour trembling.

105 *The baby of a girl*: A multiplication of unmanly types; *baby* is sometimes thought to refer to a doll.

108 *displaced*: Removed.

109 *With most admired disorder*: With this strange dis-ordering of your wits.

110 *overcome us like a summer's cloud*: Bring sudden gloom over us, as a cloud may do on a sunlit day.

111–12 *strange . . . that I owe*: Seem unlike the brave person I have supposed myself to be.

118 *Stand not upon the order of your going*: An exit in strong contrast to the entrance, III.4.1. The *disorder* in Macbeth's mind has produced social disorder.

121 *It will have blood, they say; . . . blood*: The F punc-tuation (followed here – most editors put the semi-colon before *they*) can be interpreted as an initial, half-reverie, statement of the proverb (from Genesis 9:6) followed by a more complete repetition and explanation of it.

122–5 *Stones have been known to move . . . man of blood*:
The whole of nature conspires to reveal the unnatural sin of murder.

123 *Augurs*: Prophecies.
understood relations: Either (1) reports properly
comprehended; or (2) connections elucidated.

124 *maggot-pies, and choughs*: Magpies and crows.

127 *How sayst thou, that*: What do you say to the fact
that.

130–31 *There's not a one of them . . . servant fee'd*: An explanation of how he heard *by the way*.

132 *betimes*: Either (1) early in the morning; or (2) while
there is yet time.

139 *Which must be acted . . . scanned*: There is not time
to con the part, it must be put into performance at
once.

140 *season*: Preservative.

141–2 *My strange and self-abuse . . . hard use*: My strange
self-deception (seeing Banquo's ghost) is only due
to the terror of the beginner who lacks toughening
experience.

143 *young in deed*: Novices in crime.

III.5

One of the scenes most regularly suspected of being
interpolations. Hecat is a new and hitherto unan-
nounced character, and the nature of the Witches
seems to have been changed; Macbeth is now viewed
as an adept or disciple of the Witches, not a victim.
On the other hand, the end of Hecat's speech catches
at a principal theme of the whole play, the spiritual
danger of security (see note to 32), and her speech,
though distinguished from the Witch-utterances by
its iambic (rather than trochaic) rhymes, is poeti-
cally very accomplished.

2 *beldams*: Hags.

7 *close*: Secret.

15 *Acheron*: Hell (after a river of the underworld).

21 *Unto a dismal and a fatal end*: With a view to a
disastrous and fatal conclusion.

24 *profound*: With deep or powerful qualities.

32 *security*: A key word in the play, a culpable absence of anxiety.

35 *Sing*: The full text of a song with this first line is found in the MS play *The Witch*, by Middleton, and in Davenant's version of *Macbeth*. The Davenant text of the song is far from clear, and I have been obliged to seek for light in the Middleton text. The essential matter seems to be that it is a *divided* song, with 'voices off' calling on Hecat to join them in their serial exercises. Music in the air must be heard before Hecat says *Hark! I am called*. Shakespeare's *Macbeth*, indeed, needs no more than the first two lines of the song, to be followed by Hecat's flying exit. The text of the full song given here is conflated from the Middleton and Davenant versions:

Song in the air

Come away, come away;
Hecat, Hecat, come away.

HECAT

I come, I come, I come, I come,
With all the speed I may,
With all the speed I may.
Where's Stadlin?

(IN THE AIR)

Here.

HECAT

Where's Puckle?

(IN THE AIR)

Here.
And Hoppo too, and Helwaine too.
We lack but you, we lack but you.
Come away, make up the count.

HECAT

I will but 'noint, and then I mount.

(IN THE AIR)

Here comes down one to fetch his dues,
A kiss, a coll, a sip of blood;

And why thou stay'st so long I muse,
Since the air's so sweet and good.
   A spirit like a cat descends

HECAT

O, art thou come?
What news, what news?

SPIRIT

All goes still to our delight:
Either come, or else
Refuse, refuse.

HECAT

Now I am furnished for the flight.
(*Going up*)
Now I go, now I fly,
Malkin my sweet spirit, and I.
O what a dainty pleasure 'tis
To ride in the air
When the moon shines fair,
And sing, and dance, and toy, and kiss,
Over woods, high rocks, and mountains,
Over seas, our mistress' fountains,
Over steeples, towers, and turrets,
We fly by night 'mong troops of spirits.
No ring of bells to our ears sounds,
No howls of wolves, no yelps of hounds,
No, not the noise of water's breach,
Or cannon's throat, our height can reach.
(IN THE AIR)
No ring of bells etc.

III.6

In terms of the intrigue, this scene exists to tell us
that Macbeth's purpose of sending to Macduff,
mentioned at III.4.129, has now been fulfilled; and
that Macduff has fled to England. But the speech of
Lennox serves further – as an exposé of the mind
under tyranny, reduced to irony as its sole mode of
opposition – to present the claustrophobic atmosphere
of Scotland and the scent of freedom (in the down-
right refusal of Macduff).

1–2 *My former speeches . . . interpret further*: What I have
  already said to you has matched what you think;
  and you must draw your own conclusions. (The
  whole conversation is an example of the reserve that
  must accompany tyranny.)

 2 *Only I say*: I only say.

3, 5 *gracious Duncan . . . right valiant Banquo*: No doubt
  these are Macbeth's phrases.

 10 *fact*: Crime.

 12 *pious*: (1) Religious; (2) son-like.

15–16 *For 'twould have angered any heart . . . men deny't*:
  He killed them so that men should not be angered
  by hearing them deny it.

 21 *broad words*: Unrestrained talk.

 22 *tyrant's*: Lennox is now talking *broad* himself.

 27 *the most pious Edward*: Edward the Confessor.

 28 *malevolence of fortune*: His loss of his throne.

 30 *pray the holy king, upon his aid*: Beg Edward for
  assistance.

 34 *Give to our tables meat*: Hold open feasts.

 36 *Do faithful homage and receive free honours*: The impli-
  cation is that under Macbeth the homage paid to the
  sovereign is hypocritical, the honours not *free*, but
  bought by servility.

 37 *this report*: If the *King* at 38 is Macbeth (see note
  on that line) then the report might be (a) that of
  Macduff's flight or (b) that of Malcolm's reception
  in England. The syntax would suggest (a); but this
  has the disadvantage of contradicting IV.1.141
  (where Macbeth appears ignorant of Macduff's
  flight) and it seems preferable to understand (b)
  here. We may, if we wish, imagine that Shakespeare's
  original draft ran straight on from *respect* (29) to
  And (37).

 38 *the*: F's reading *their* suggests that the *King* is Edward;
  and this would make perfect sense as far as the
  Lord's speech is concerned. But the *he* of Lennox's
  reply must be Macbeth; and if this is so, the *King*
  must also be Macbeth.

40–41 *And with an absolute 'Sir, not I!' . . . his back*: The
messenger turns back towards his master, bearing
Macduff's *absolute not I* answer.

41 *cloudy*: Lowering, scowling.

   me: Ethic dative; only present to give emphasis.

42 *hums*: Says 'hum' ('um', 'umph').

43 *clogs*: Impedes my advancement. (Messengers bearing
bad news did not recommend themselves to tyrants.)

44 *him*: Macduff.

   distance: Between himself and Macbeth.

IV.1

Usually set in a cavern, because of the *pit of Acheron*
reference at III.5.15; but 46 seems to imply a building
with a door. The scene bears the same (generative)
relationship to the second half of the play as do the
prophecies of I.3 to the first half. The iambic
speeches, 39–43, 124–31, are often thought inter-
polated; they exist to justify the song and dance,
and obviously differ in their tone – more delicate
and pleasant – from the rest of the Witch material.

1 *brinded cat*: Streaked cat (the First Witch's familiar).

2 *hedge-pig*: Hedgehog.

3 *Harpier*: The third familiar – a word formed from
'Harpy'.

7 *thirty-one*: Meaning, I suppose, 'one full month'.

8 *Sweltered venom, sleeping got*: Venom sweated out
during sleep.

10, etc. *Double, double, toil and trouble*: Let toil and trouble
be doubled in the world.

12 *fenny*: Living in fen or marshland.

15 *tongue of dog*: Appears in this sinister catalogue
because of Shakespeare's abhorrence of canine
fawning.

16 *fork*: Forked tongue.

   blind-worm: Slow-worm (now known to be venom-
less).

17 *howlet*: Young owl.

18 *For*: In order to produce.

19 *boil and bubble*: Imperatives.

23 *Witch's mummy*: Mummified fragments of a witch.
   maw and gulf: Gullet and stomach.

24 *ravined*: Having finished devouring his prey.

25 *digged i'the dark*: At the time when it was most
   noxious.

26 *Liver*: Supposed to be the seat of the passions.
   blaspheming: Because a *Jew* denies Christ's divinity.

27 *Gall*: Secretion of the liver; rancour.
   slips: Seedlings.
   yew: Because poisonous.

28 *Slivered in the moon's eclipse*: Torn from the tree at
   a particularly baneful time.

29 *Turk . . . Tartar*: Like *Jew* (26) and *babe* (30), attractive to witches because unchristened.

31 *Ditch-delivered by a drab*: Born in a ditch, the child
   of a harlot.

32 *slab*: Viscous.

33 *chaudron*: Entrails.

34 *cauldron*: The Elizabethan pronunciation of *cauldron*
   (as of *vault*, *falcon*, *caulk*, etc.) kept the 'l' silent,
   so that the rhyme with *chaudron* was perfect.

37 *baboon's blood*: Hot and lustful; and therefore only
   cooling to the unnaturally fiery (*baboon* has accent
   on first syllable).

38 *Enter Hecat and the other three Witches*: The song
   'Black spirits' (as it appears in Middleton's *The Witch*)
   does not require more than three performers, though
   the refrain might be thought to deserve a larger
   body. If a chorus of six witches seems offensive we
   can read (as is sometimes done): 'Enter Hecat [to]
   the other three Witches', and so avoid increasing
   the witch population.

43 *a song*: The full text of a song with this first line
   is found in the MS play *The Witch*, by Middleton,
   and in Davenant's printed version of *Macbeth*; I
   quote the latter version, in which particular references to the plot of *The Witch* have been deleted:

HECATE

Black spirits, and white,
Red spirits, and grey,
Mingle, mingle, mingle,
You that mingle may.

FIRST WITCH

Tiffin, Tiffin, keep it stiff in;
Firedrake, Puckey, make it lucky;
Liar Robin, you must bob in.

CHORUS

Around, around, about, about;
All ill come running in, all good keep out.

FIRST WITCH

Here's the blood of a bat.

HECATE

O, put in that, put in that.

SECOND WITCH

Here's lizard's brain.

HECATE

Put in a grain.

FIRST WITCH

Here's juice of toad, here's oil of adder;
That will make the charm grow madder.

SECOND WITCH

Put in all these, 'twill raise the stench.

HECATE

Nay, here's three ounces of a red-haired wench.

CHORUS

Around, around, about, about;
All ill come running in, all good keep out.

47 *secret, black, and midnight hags*: Wicked practitioners
   of 'black' magic.

51–9 *Though you untie the winds . . . till destruction sicken*:
   Though order, civilization and the cosmos itself be
   destroyed.

51 *Though you untie the winds*: Cf. Revelation 7:1: 'I
   saw four angels stand on the four corners of the
   earth, holding back the four winds of the earth . . .'

52 *yesty*: Foaming.

54 *bladed corn be lodged*: New corn be beaten flat.

57–8 *the treasure . . . tumble all together*: The patterns of creation fall into confusion.

58 *nature's germens*: The seeds or material essences of things.

59 *Even till destruction sicken*: Through over-eating.

62 *masters*: The powers of Fate.

67 *Thyself and office*: Thyself performing thy function.
   an Armed Head: Presumably that of Macbeth himself, cut off by Macduff. The same property head would suffice for both occasions.

73 *harped*: Guessed.

75 *a Bloody Child*: Presumably Macduff, *from his mother's womb | Untimely ripped* (V.6.54–5).

83 *take a bond of fate*: A *bond* to *make assurance double sure* – by disposing of Macduff (and the First Apparition's warning) *and* relying on *none of woman born* (79).

85 *thunder*: Traditionally the expression of God's anger.
   a Child Crowned, with a tree in his hand: Malcolm, advancing with a branch of *Birnan Wood*.

92 *Birnan*: F has *Byrnam* here; the correct form in modern geography is 'Birnam'. But Elizabethan authorities spell the word with an 'n' ('Bernane' in Holinshed; 'Brynnane' in Wintoun's *Original Chronicle*); and this is the form F uses on every other occasion when the name appears (IV.1.97; V.3.2, 60; V.4.3; V.5.34, 44; V.6.69). We must assume that the 'm' is an error here, and that *Birnan* is the correct Shakespearian form.

93–101 *That will never be . . . Can tell so much*: As Kittredge notes, Macbeth's continuation of the rhymed speech-form of the Apparition implies his absorption into that world of false 'security'. Note also his third-person reference to himself (97).

94 *impress*: Conscript.

95 *bodements*: Auguries.

96 *Rebellious dead*: Theobald's emendation 'Rebellion's

head' has been generally accepted. It takes up, very neatly, the idea of *where conspirers are* (90). But the idea of *dead* is much closer to *Unfix . . . root*, which can be seen to resurrect, in Macbeth's mind, the obsession with Banquo that runs through the scene. Banquo's ghost is a type of the rebellious – *But now they rise . . . And push us from our stools* (III.4.79–81).

99 *mortal custom*: The custom of dying.

110 *eight kings, and Banquo*: Banquo was supposed to be the ancestor of the Stuart line. The eight kings would be Robert II, Robert III, James I, James II, James III, James IV, James V, Mary Queen of Scots. If we exclude Mary we have to include Walter Stewart (preceding Robert II).

116 *What, will the line stretch out to the crack of doom*: The Stuarts were proud of their unbroken lineal descent.

118 *a glass*: Supposed to reflect the figure of James I, the principal spectator of the play.

120 *That two-fold balls . . . carry*: Unite the crowns of England and Scotland (*two-fold*) and rule over Scotland, England and Ireland (*treble*) – as did James I.

122 *blood-boltered*: His hair matted with blood.

123 *for his*: Claiming them as his descendants.

131 *The Witches dance*: This has been thought to be a further borrowing of music from *The Witch*, where we read 'here they dance the Witches' dance, and Exit'.

144–5 *The flighty purpose . . . go with it*: We never realize our quickly vanishing purposes, unless we act at the very moment when we form these purposes.

148 *it*: What follows.

152 *trace*: Follow his tracks.

154 *these gentlemen*: The *two or three* of 140.

IV.2

The scene breaks the grim descent of Macbeth by an interlude of domestic pathos. Both Ross and the nameless Messenger represent the natural sympathy of the oppressed under devilish pressure; their flight catches the weakness of any amiable ordinary individual under these circumstances and mirrors that of Macduff himself. Notice the descent from the 'honourable' murderers of Banquo to the brutish ruffians of this scene.

3–4   *when our actions . . . traitors*: Macduff had *done* nothing traitorous; but his fear made him fly, and that is treachery.

10   *diminutive*: F uses the alternative form *diminitive*, the sound of which may be thought more appropriate to the meaning of the line.

11   *Her young ones in her nest*: When her young ones are in the nest.

14   *cuz*: Cousin, relative.

15   *school yourself*: Teach yourself wisdom.

17   *The fits o'the season*: The unexpected convulsions of this time; ? what is fitting.

18–19   *when we are traitors . . . ourselves*: When we are proclaimed as traitors and ourselves do not know that we are.

19–20   *when we hold rumour | From what we fear*: When all we have to hold on to are rumours, based on what we fear might be.

22   *Each way and move*: The sense must be that the ignorantly fearful are at the mercy of the sea of fear; and are moved whatever way the sea moves. The language is not easy to fit into this; nor is the favourite emendation, 'Each way and none.'

29   *It would be my disgrace and your discomfort*: I should weep and so disgrace my manhood and distress you.

31   *Sirrah*: Playful and affectionate address here.

36   *lime*: Birdlime (a sticky substance spread on branches, etc., to catch birds).
      gin: Snare.

37   *Poor birds they are not set for*: Traps, etc., are not set for a *poor* bird (as you call me, 35).

42   *Then you'll buy 'em to sell again*: You can't want all that number for your own consumption.

43–4 *Thou speak'st with all thy wit . . . for thee*: You're
      not being very sensible; but sensible enough, I
      suppose, considering your age.

48 *swears and lies*: Takes an oath and breaks it. (Lady
      Macduff is thinking of the marriage-oath to cherish
      the wife, as well as the oath to the King.)

59 *monkey*: 'Used tenderly, in the fantasticality of
      affection' (Kittredge).

66 *in your state of honour I am perfect*: I am perfectly
      acquainted with your honourable condition.

71–2 *To do worse to you were fell cruelty . . . your person*:
      It would be cruel to do more than frighten (i.e.
      harm) you, but such cruelty is close at hand.

78 *womanly*: Womanish, feeble.

80 *Where is your husband*: Coming from Macbeth, they
      must know that he is fled; but the Gestapo-type
      question may serve to incriminate Lady Macduff.

82, 83 *thou*: Pejorative use of second person singular.

84 *fry*: Fish-spawn.

IV.3

This, the longest scene in the play, performs a number
of important structural functions. Of the three
sections: (a) Malcolm's testing of Macduff, (b) the
description of Edward the Confessor and (c) the
announcement of the slaughter of Macduff's family,
the first is the most elaborate. It adds a further strand
to the image of wariness and suspiciousness that
characterizes tyranny. Malcolm's self-accusations
describe the contrast between virtue and vice in king-
ship and Macduff's reactions are those of the ideal
subject. Pious Edward touching for 'the Evil' is
directly antithetical to Macbeth, and the Doctor here
should be contrasted with that in V.1. Macduff's
reaction to Ross's bitter news exhibits full human
range of feeling, of understanding and resolve to
act. With piety to crown the effort, and with resolve
to carry it forward, the countermove against Macbeth
is fully launched.

3 *mortal*: Deadly.

4 *Bestride our down-fallen birthdom*: Stand over and defend the fallen body of the kingdom of our birth.

6 *Strike heaven on the face*: Are as a slap in the face of goodness.

6–8 *that it resounds . . . Like syllable of dolour*: The noise of the blow against heaven echoes as if heaven were wailing for sorrow, like Scotland.

10 *to friend*: Favourable.

14 *I am young; but*: (1) Although I am unimportant; (2) although I may seem innocent, I can understand that.

15 *wisdom*: It is wisdom.

19–20 *recoil . . . charge*: Be pushed backwards (morally) by the force of a royal command (image from gunnery).

21 *transpose*: Change (suspicion cannot make Macduff evil).

22 *the brightest*: Lucifer.

24 *so*: Like grace.

25 *Perchance even there where I did find my doubts*: Macduff left his family in Macbeth's power. Was the betrayal of Malcolm to be the price of their safety? It was this thought that alerted Malcolm's *doubts*; and so Macduff will have to give up *hope* of recovering his family.

26 *rawness*: Unprotected condition.

27 *motives*: (1) Incentives to action; (2) objects moving one's emotions.

29 *jealousies*: Suspicions.

32–3 *tyranny . . . thou . . . thou*: Macbeth.

34 *affeered*: Legally confirmed.

37 *to boot*: As well.

43 *gracious England*: Edward the Confessor, full of God's grace.

52 *opened*: As a bud opens – after *grafted*.

56, 57 *devil . . . evils*: Both monosyllables.

57 *top*: Surpass.

58 *Luxurious*: Lustful.

59 *Sudden*: Violent.

64 *continent*: (1) Chaste; (2) restraining.

65 *will*: Lust.

67 *nature*: Human nature.

71 *Convey*: Manage secretly.

72 *hoodwink*: Blindfold.

75 *greatness*: The great man, King Malcolm.

76 *so*: So lustfully.

77 *ill-composed affection*: Disposition composed of evil elements.

78 *staunchless*: Unquenchable.

80 *his*: One man's.

81–2 *And my more-having . . . make me hunger more*: The more I swallowed up, the sharper my appetite should be.

82 *that*: So that.

86 *summer-seeming*: That beseems or befits the summer of life (early manhood).

88 *foisons*: Abundance.
   will: Passion.

89 *Of your mere own*: Out of your own royal possessions.
   portable: Bearable.

93 *perseverance*: Accented on the second syllable.

95–6 *abound . . . each several crime*: I am fertile in the variations that can be produced in each separate (*several*) crime.

98 *milk*: Symbolizing, as already in the play, the innocence of natural relationships.

99 *Uproar*: Reduce to confusion.

104 *untitled*: With no legal right.

107 *accused*: F's *accust* may also be modernized as 'accursed'.

108 *does blaspheme his breed*: Is a slander to his family.

111 *Died every day she lived*: Mortified herself daily (by religious exercises).

113 *breast*: Heart.

115 *Child of integrity*: Produced by the integrity of your spirit.

116 *black scruples*: Wicked suspicions.

118 *trains*: Lures.

126 *Unknown to woman*: A virgin.

131 *upon*: Against.

135 *at a point*: Fully prepared.

136–7 *and the chance of goodness . . . quarrel*: May the chance of good success be proportionate to the justness of our cause.

142–3 *convinces | The great assay of art*: Defeats the greatest efforts of medical skill.

143–5 *but at his touch . . . They presently amend*: This is 'touching' for scrofula or 'the King's Evil', which began with Edward the Confessor and remained a prerogative of the English crown.

145 *presently*: Immediately.

152 *mere*: Complete.

153 *stamp*: Coin.

160 *My countryman . . . I know him not*: Malcolm presumably recognizes the 'Scottish' costume Ross is wearing.

162 *betimes*: Speedily.

166–7 *nothing | But who knows nothing*: No one except a person totally ignorant.

169 *not marked*: Not noticed, because they are everywhere.

170 *modern ecstasy*: Commonplace passion.

173 *or ere they sicken*: Before they have time to fall ill.

174 *Too nice*: Over-delicately phrased.

175 *doth hiss the speaker*: Causes him to be hissed (because the news is out of date).

176 *teems*: Brings forth plenteously.

177 *well . . . Well*: Because 'we use | To say the dead are well' (*Antony and Cleopatra*, II.5.32–3).

181–2 *the tidings . . . heavily borne*: Is this the 'heavy' (sad) news of Macduff's family?

183 *out*: In arms.

188 *doff*: Take off.

189 *Gracious England*: Edward the Confessor.

191 *none*: There are none.

192 *gives out*: Proclaims.

195 *latch*: Catch.

196–7 *fee-grief . . . single breast*: Grief with a single owner.

206 *quarry*: Heap of dead animals.

208 *pull your hat*: A conventional sign of grief.

215 *deadly*: Which would otherwise be fatal.

217 *hell-kite*: That swooped on his *chickens* like a bird from hell.

219 *Dispute*: Struggle against.

224 *for thee*: Because of thee. (Heaven would have intervened if Macduff's wickedness had not dissuaded it.) *Naught*: Wicked.

231 *intermission*: Interval of time.

236 *Our lack . . . our leave*: We lack nothing but leavetaking.

237 *ripe for shaking*: Perhaps a reminiscence from Nahum's prophecy of the fall of Nineveh: 'All thy strong aids are as fig trees with the first ripe figs: if they be stirred, they fall into the mouth of the eater' (Nahum 3:12).

238 *Put on their instruments*: (1) Put on their weapons; (2) thrust us forward, as their agents.

V.I

The scene re-enacts the life of bloodshed in terms of dream and hallucination (like a Noh play). It is the climax of Shakespeare's exploration of individual psychological secrets. The broken prose fragments of Lady Macbeth's speech measure the collapse of the human mind under inhuman pressures, while the Gentlewoman and the Doctor represent a choric norm. The Doctor (probably played by the same actor as the Doctor in IV.3) serves to focus the contrast between the English throne with its heaven-given medical powers, and the Scottish with its disease *beyond my practice* (55).

5 *nightgown*: The Elizabethans slept without garments; the *nightgown* was equivalent to today's dressing-gown. Re-enacts II.2.70.

8 *while*: Time.

9–10 *A great perturbation in nature . . . watching*: Lady Macbeth 'equivocates' with sleep.

10 *watching*: Waking.

17–18 *having no witness to confirm my speech*: The Waiting-Gentlewoman is as suspicious as other subjects of tyranny.

31 *Yet*: 'After all this washing' (Kittredge).

34 *One: two*: Lady Macbeth recalls the timing of Duncan's murder.

35 *do't*: Murder Duncan.
    Hell is murky: 'A sudden glimpse into the abyss at her feet' (Dover Wilson).

42 *will these hands ne'er be clean*: This recalls (as so much of this scene does) *A little water clears us of this deed; | How easy is it then!* (II.2.67–8).

50 *charged*: Burdened.

63–4 *What's done cannot be undone*: A tragically ironic echo of *what's done is done* (III.2.12).

66 *Directly*: Immediately.

67–8 *unnatural deeds . . . troubles*: Rebellion is *unnatural*, but is naturally produced when sovereigns commit *unnatural* deeds.

72 *Remove from her the means of all annoyance*: Lady Macbeth is in a state of Despair (religiously conceived), and therefore must be considered a potential suicide.

74 *mated*: Confounded.

V.2

4 *alarm*: The call to battle.

10 *unrough*: Beardless.

11 *Protest their first of manhood*: Proclaim that they are now (for the first time) acting as men.

15 *distempered*: Diseased; perhaps 'swollen with dropsy'.

17 *sticking*: Like dried blood.

18 *minutely*: Occurring every minute (accented on first syllable).

19 *in*: Because of.

22–3 *blame . . . and start*: Blame his afflicted nerves for jumping back and quivering.

24–5 *When all that is within him . . . being there*: When his whole nature revolts against his existence.

27 *medicine*: (1) Drug; or more probably (2) physician
(i.e. Malcolm).
sickly weal: The diseased commonwealth.

28–9 *And with him pour . . . Each drop of us*: As men
purge their disorders by bloodletting, so let us pour
out our blood (in battle) to purge *the sickly weal*.

30 *sovereign*: (1) Royal; (2) powerfully medicinal.

V.3

The desperate 'security' of Macbeth, without hope,
without companionship and therefore without
meaning in his life – this is represented externally
by the siege and internally by his despair. The Doctor
serves, once again, to link the state of the mind
with the state of the land, psychology with politics.

1 *them*: The thanes.

8 *English epicures*: From the traditional Scottish point
of view the English are characterized by luxurious
softness.

9 *sway*: Rule myself.

11 *damn thee black*: Damned souls were thought to be
black in colour.

12 *goose look*: Look of cowardly folly.

14 *prick thy face and over-red thy fear*: Stick pins in your
face and let the blood hide your pallor.

15 *lily-livered*: Lacking in red-blooded bravery.
patch: Fool.

16 *linen*: Bleached.

20 *push*: Crisis.

21 *chair*: Printed in F as *cheere*; the two words were
pronounced alike; but *chair* seems the more apposite word to keep in line with *push* and *dis-seat*.

23 *sere, the yellow leaf*: A withered condition.

27–8 *breath . . . would fain deny*: Words of allegiance which
the emotions cannot accept as true – as in 'equivocation'. Cf. Isaiah 29:13: 'this people when they be
in trouble do honour me with their mouth and with
their lips, but their heart is far from me . . .'

35 *more*: F prints the alternative Elizabethan form *moe*.
skirr: Scour.

37 *your patient*: The *your* is emphatic, to make the contrast between Macbeth's treatment of the realm and the Doctor's of Lady Macbeth – a contrast that recurs at 47–8 and 50–54.

38 *thick-coming*: Frequently appearing.

42 *written*: Engraved.

44 *stuffed*: Clogged (Kittredge notes the clogged movement of the line).

48 *staff*: Baton of office.

50–51 *cast* | *The water*: Examine the urine.

55 *senna*: F reads *Cyme*; and this has been found in English, as an Anglicization of Greek/Latin '*cyma*', the tender shoots of plants. But I suspect that the appearance of this rare word in F is an accident, and that Shakespeare's word was 'cynne' – a variant spelling of *senna* – which has the right meaning and the right value for scansion.

56 *scour*: (1) Remove rapidly (as *skirr*, 35); (2) cleanse the body by purgatives; (3) also used of cleaning armour.

58 *it*: The piece of armour.

62 *Profit*: The traditional motive of doctors.

V.4

Now all the nobles we have known from earlier in the play have joined Malcolm's army. Notice the humility of their grasp on the future, to be compared with Macbeth's furious indifference.

2 *chambers*: Perhaps bed-chambers – they were not safe for Duncan.

5 *shadow*: Conceal.

6 *discovery*: Spying.

10 *setting down before't*: Besieging it.

11 *there is advantage to be given*: Opportunity (to escape) is afforded them.

12 *more and less*: Great men and humble men.

14–15 *Let our just censures . . . event*: If our judgements are to be accurate, they must wait to know the true end of the affair.

18 *What we shall say we have, and what we owe*: The

difference between talk and true possession (*owe* = own).

20 *But certain issue strokes must arbitrate*: Only blows decide the real future.

V.5

The alternation of scenes in Act V makes this a natural extension of V.3. The supreme horror of the heart numbed by despair appears in the reaction to Lady Macbeth's death. From this time forth Macbeth's life is a waiting for the end.

5 *farced*: Stuffed. F's *forc'd* is sometimes defended as having the sense of 'reinforced'; but this meaning is only doubtfully attested. In view of the food images in the line before it seems best to take *forc'd* as the common Elizabethan variant of *farced*.

6 *dareful*: In open battle.

10 *cooled*: Chilled with terror.

11 *my fell of hair*: The hair on my skin.

12 *dismal treatise*: A story of disaster.

13 *supped full with*: Had my fill of. The metaphor takes us back to III.4.

14 *familiar*: Is there a reminiscence here of the Witches' familiars?

17 *should*: I think this means 'certainly would' rather than 'ought to have'.
   hereafter: At some time – what does the actual moment matter?

18 *There would have been a time for such a word*: His mind moves back from the meaninglessness of any future to the meaningfulness of the past – 'At one time I could have responded to such a word (announcement)'. The transition to the following line implies the transition from that past to this present.

20 *in this petty pace*: In the petty manner of this pace. I assume that he paces as he speaks.

21 *To the last syllable of recorded time*: Till time reaches the last recorded word.

23 *dusty death*: Death, which is a matter of 'dust to dust'.

24 *shadow*: Suggested by *lighted . . . candle* and suggesting *player* in its turn. Cf. Job 8:9: 'we are but of yesterday . . . our days upon earth are but a shadow.'

   a poor player: The actor is *poor* (i.e. worthy of pity) because his voice soon ceases to be heard.

25 *frets*: Expresses discontent and disdain.

40 *cling*: Shrink up, wither.

   sooth: True.

42 *pull in*: Rein in. (Many editors have preferred to emend to 'pall in'.)

V.6

   Usually printed as four separate scenes, but logic would demand either more divisions (e.g. at 23 and 73) or none at all. The battle is a series of spotlights but the action must be continuous. The alternation between sides that has marked Act V so far now speeds up, till the two blur into one victory and one defeat.

2 *uncle*: Seyward.

4 *battle*: Battalion.

   we: Malcolm now assumes the royal *we*.

10 *harbingers*: Forerunners.

11 *They have tied me to a stake*: Like a bear being baited.

12 *the course*: One round of dogs vs. a bear.

30 *undeeded*: Without any deeds performed.

34 *gently rendered*: Surrendered without fighting.

39 *strike beside us*: Miss intentionally.

40 *the Roman fool*: Some Stoic suicide – e.g. Brutus.

48 *intrenchant*: That cannot be gashed.

53 *angel*: Demon.

   still: Always.

58 *juggling*: Deceiving, cheating.

59 *palter with us in a double sense*: Equivocate by double meanings.

64 *monsters*: Prodigies, marvels.

65 *Painted upon a pole*: On a painted cloth set up on a pole (in front of the booth).

71 *try the last*: Make the final test (of fate).

73 *Exeunt fighting . . . Enter fighting, and Macbeth slain*:
It is not clear why F has these two contradictory
directions. Perhaps they *Exeunt* from the main stage
and then *Enter* on the inner stage (or balcony) where
a curtain can be drawn to conceal Macbeth's body.
Retreat: The trumpet-call for the end of the fighting.

75 *go off*: Die (perhaps a stage metaphor = exit).

87 *hairs*: With pun on 'heirs'.

91 *parted*: Departed.
score: Reckoning, account.

93 *stands*: Presumably the head is on a pole.

95 *pearl*: Suggested probably by the idea of 'peers' and
by the pearls which surround a crown.

100 *reckon with your several loves*: Add up what we owe
to each individual.

102 *Scotland*: ?The King of Scotland.

104 *Which would be planted newly with the time*: Which
ought to be given a new beginning in a new age.

107 *ministers*: Agents.

109 *by self and violent hands*: By her own violent hands.

111 *by the grace of Grace*: With God's help.

112 *measure . . . place*: With due order in every
dimension.

The National: three theatres and so much more...
www.nationaltheatre.org.uk

In its three theatres on London's South Bank, the National presents an eclectic mix of new plays and classics, with seven or eight shows in repertory at any one time.

And there's more. Step inside and enjoy free exhibitions, backstage tours, talks and readings, a great theatre bookshop and plenty of places to eat and drink.

Sign-up as an e-member at www.nationaltheatre.org.uk/join and we'll keep you up-to-date with everything that's going on.

NATIONAL THEATRE
SOUTH BANK
LONDON SE1 9PX

PENGUIN SHAKESPEARE

CYMBELINE
WILLIAM SHAKESPEARE

WWW.PENGUINSHAKESPEARE.COM

The King of Britain, enraged by his daughter's disobedience in
marrying against his wishes, banishes his new son-in-law. Having fled
to Rome, the exiled husband makes a foolish wager with a villain he
encounters there – gambling on the fidelity of his abandoned wife.
Combining courtly menace and horror, comedy and melodrama,
Cymbeline is a moving depiction of two young lovers driven apart by
deceit and self-doubt.

This book includes a general introduction to Shakespeare's life and the
Elizabethan theatre, a separate introduction to *Cymbeline*, a chronology
of his works, suggestions for further reading, an essay discussing
performance options on both stage and screen, and a commentary.

Edited with an introduction by John Pitcher

General Editor: Stanley Wells

PENGUIN SHAKESPEARE

HAMLET
WILLIAM SHAKESPEARE

WWW.PENGUINSHAKESPEARE.COM

A young Prince meets with his father's ghost, who alleges that his own brother, now married to his widow, murdered him. The Prince devises a scheme to test the truth of the ghost's accusation, feigning wild madness while plotting a brutal revenge. But his apparent insanity soon begins to wreak havoc on innocent and guilty alike.

This book includes a general introduction to Shakespeare's life and the Elizabethan theatre, a separate introduction to *Hamlet*, a chronology of his works, suggestions for further reading, an essay discussing performance options on both stage and screen by Paul Prescott, and a commentary.

Edited by T. J. B. Spencer

With an introduction by Alan Sinfield

General Editor: Stanley Wells

PENGUIN SHAKESPEARE

KING LEAR
WILLIAM SHAKESPEARE

WWW.PENGUINSHAKESPEARE.COM

An ageing king makes a capricious decision to divide his realm among his three daughters according to the love they express for him. When the youngest daughter refuses to take part in this charade, she is banished, leaving the king dependent on her manipulative and untrustworthy sisters. In the scheming and recriminations that follow, not only does the king's own sanity crumble, but the stability of the realm itself is also threatened.

This book includes a general introduction to Shakespeare's life and the Elizabethan theatre, a separate introduction to *King Lear*, a chronology of his works, suggestions for further reading, an essay discussing performance options on both stage and screen, and a commentary.

Edited by George Hunter

With an introduction by Kiernan Ryan

General Editor: Stanley Wells

Penguin Shakespeare

OTHELLO
WILLIAM SHAKESPEARE

WWW.PENGUINSHAKESPEARE.COM

A popular soldier and newly married man, Othello seems to be in an enviable position. And yet, when his supposed friend sows doubts in his mind about his wife's fidelity, he is gradually consumed by suspicion. In this powerful tragedy, innocence is corrupted and trust is eroded as every relationship is drawn into a tangled web of jealousies.

This book includes a general introduction to Shakespeare's life and the Elizabethan theatre, a separate introduction to *Othello*, a chronology of his works, suggestions for further reading, an essay discussing performance options on both stage and screen, and a commentary.

Edited by Kenneth Muir

With an introduction by Tom McAlindon

General Editor: Stanley Wells

PENGUIN SHAKESPEARE

RICHARD III
WILLIAM SHAKESPEARE

WWW.PENGUINSHAKESPEARE.COM

The bitter, deformed brother of the King is secretly plotting to seize the throne of England. Charming and duplicitous, powerfully eloquent and viciously cruel, he is prepared to go to any lengths to achieve his goal – and, in his skilful manipulation of events and people, Richard is a chilling incarnation of the lure of evil and the temptation of power.

This book includes a general introduction to Shakespeare's life and the Elizabethan theatre, a separate introduction to *Richard III*, a chronology of his works, suggestions for further reading, an essay discussing performance options on both stage and screen by Gillian Day, and a commentary.

Edited by E. A. J. Honigmann

With an introduction by Michael Taylor

General Editor: Stanley Wells

PENGUIN SHAKESPEARE

ROMEO AND JULIET
WILLIAM SHAKESPEARE

WWW.PENGUINSHAKESPEARE.COM

A young man and woman meet by chance and fall instantly in love. But their families are bitter enemies, and in order to be together the two lovers must be prepared to risk everything. Set in a city torn apart by feuds and gang warfare, *Romeo and Juliet* is a dazzling combination of passion and hatred, bawdy comedy and high tragedy.

This book includes a general introduction to Shakespeare's life and the Elizabethan theatre, a separate introduction to *Romeo and Juliet*, a chronology of his works, suggestions for further reading, an essay discussing performance options on both stage and screen, and a commentary.

Edited by T. J. B. Spencer

With an introduction by Adrian Poole

General Editor: Stanley Wells

PENGUIN SHAKESPEARE

KING JOHN
WILLIAM SHAKESPEARE

WWW.PENGUINSHAKESPEARE.COM

Under the rule of King John, England is forced into war when the French challenge the legitimacy of John's claim to the throne and determine to install his nephew Arthur in his place. But political principles, hypocritically flaunted, are soon forgotten, as the French and English kings form an alliance based on cynical self-interest. And as the desire to cling to power dominates England's paranoid and weak-willed king, his country is threatened with disaster.

This book includes a general introduction to Shakespeare's life and the Elizabethan theatre, a separate introduction to *King John*, a chronology of his works, suggestions for further reading, an essay discussing performance options on both stage and screen, and a commentary.

Edited by R. L. Smallwood

With an introduction by Eugene Giddens

General Editor: Stanley Wells

Read more in Penguin

PENGUIN SHAKESPEARE